Vera Kara's Family

Picking Up the Pieces, Again!

Vera Kara's Family

Picking Up the Pieces, Again!

BY

AGNES "AGGIE" HANNES

LUCIDBOOKS

Vera Kara's Family

Copyright © 2011 by Agnes Hannes

Published by Lucid Books in Brenham, TX.
www.LucidBooks.net

First Printing 2011

ISBN-13: 9781935909279
ISBN-10: 1935909274

Special Sales: Most Lucid Books titles are available in special quantity discounts. Custom imprinting or excerpting can also be done to fit special needs. Contact Lucid Books at info@lucidbooks.net.

Contents

Foreword

Over twenty years ago in a local paper, I read a short version of this story written by Vera and somehow could not shake the story from my mind. It was like an obsession; I felt the story was so compelling and interesting that the entire story needed to be told. I have been working on it off and on for more than eight years. The complexity of the story and its entwinement in recognizable and obscure historical events left me so many contributing situations and events to understand and relate to the story. I have finally decided I have to write what I know from my extensive interviews with Vera and her son and the information I have compiled, or I could continue researching for the rest of my life.

The core events in the stories are based on actual events in the Kara family history (pronounced Car-a), but the day-to-day account is my interpretation based on interviews and research. Vera shared such in-depth insight into the personalities of her ancestors and her family that I feel I knew them personally. Very few of the stories about the hardship they endured on the escape through Siberia were ever shared with Vera. From what they did tell her, she knew it was terrible and the wolves were vicious and plentiful. Her parents just wanted to forget it ever happened. Vera did not know the route they had taken from Russia to Harbin, China. The wolf story is the only event in the book that is not based on the Kara family history, but there is no doubt their journey was rigorous and similar hardships were endured by many of the Russian refugees along the escape routes to China. I found a wealth of general information about customs and history of Germans in Russia from http://www.volgagermans.net. Before I did this research, I knew nothing of these fine hard working people with such rich heritage.

Some of the family in this story asked to remain anonymous to protect their children's confidentiality; so many of the names and places in the book have been changed to honor that request. I found this difficult to do because their original names were perfect for their personalities and how they lived. Any similarity in the names I have given the family members to anyone alive or deceased is purely coincidental. Vera did not know names of anyone her ancestors encountered along the escape route. Also the name Igor Ivanson, the leader of the Communist movement in Saratov, is totally fictitious. Vera never knew the man's name, just his deeds, so any similarity in name to anyone living or deceased is purely coincidental.

I got to know and love Vera when she was living in Central Texas and married to her 4th husband. My husband and I were privileged to experience one of her fabulous sit-down dinner parties, and I can say it was truly "second to none." For our interviews, many times we went to Chinese restaurants, and when Vera talked to the waiters and owners in Chinese, we got very special treatment. She was a joy to know. The memory of the laughter we shared in the interviews made writing this story a labor of love.

I invite you to look at the pictures from the Kara family photo album in the middle of this book.

Dedication

To my loving husband, Lummus Arnold Hannes,
the finest man I have ever met.
Without your help and encouragement,
this book would never have been completed.

To my special grandson, Colton Chase Stahl.
Your continual excitement for and interest in my book
has been a significant driving force for me.

To Brad Bevers, my publisher, and Laura Jackson, my editor,
for making this such a pleasant experience.

To the Lord Jesus Christ, thank you for your
guidance and blessings.

Vera Kara's Family
Picking Up the Pieces, Again!

As Anton waits for his family to gather for breakfast, his mind is in turmoil, wishing he could turn back the hands of time. After so many years, he still misses Martha, their precious little girl. All her laughter, funny stories, and hugs are gone forever. To keep her close, he and Laura, his beloved wife, buried their little girl on the far side of Laura's rose garden here on the grounds of their estate. Martha's grave was the first grave in the new family plot. As he looks across the roses from the window of the breakfast nook, he sees two graves and knows beyond a shadow of a doubt that his broken heart will never mend.

Last year Laura had unexpectedly taken ill in the middle of the night and died before dawn, joining their daughter in that cold ground at the edge of her rose garden. Now he feels so alone, so inadequate to lead the family without the help of his best friend and confidant. He feels he has decisions to make, but then maybe he is just an old man blowing things out of proportions. He needs someone to talk to this morning.

Anton's youngest son Alois is the first to join his father at the breakfast table. He is the most outgoing one of the three, now grown, young men Anton and Laura raised with such love and devotion. At 17, Alois enjoys being the son of the owner of the Saratov Brewing Co. here in Southwestern Russia. Alois is a handsome young man with wavy brown hair and a spark of mischief in his dark blue eyes. His masculinity is underscored by his height. Despite his young age, he is already much taller than most grown men. His features are small for a man of his height, creating a smooth and refined appearance especially attractive to the ladies. With an expansive outlook on life, he is always questioning conventional wisdom and exploring new ideas with an exuberance only youth can produce on such a continual basis. He has both male and female friends in abundance, but he is especially attracted to beautiful, frivolous young women. He loves to debate ideas and issues whether he believes in them or not.

Of late, Alois has been bringing home political ideas Anton does not support. Anton always listens attentively to the new concepts because he knows if he takes issue with anything, a debate will develop that Alois will relish and Anton will hate. Anton could pass the ideas off as silly immature banter; however, he has heard the same ideas being discussed everywhere he goes here in the valley.

The Germans living here in the Volga River Valley don't agree with the new idea that personal ownership of property is not in the best interest of society. Most of the locals, and their families before them, have spent their whole lives working hard for a better life by being innovative and frugal. The new concept will take from the people who have and share it with the people who don't have. Since Anton's family, the Karas, are some of the haves because of their hard work, the idea isn't sitting well at all.

Many of the people comprising this productive area are direct descendants of the first people to come to this valley. A little more than a century ago, Catherine the Great visited Germany to invite and encourage people to come settle in this area and make it productive. The Germans did this by building irrigation ditches and implementing innovative concepts in their crop production. The immigrants had been promised by the Czarina's land agents a land of milk and honey, housing, and tools. When they arrived, they found a wolf-infested wilderness with no housing, no tools, but rich land. They made the best of an awful situation. Up until the present time, the basic promise made by the Czarina to leave the people alone to take care of their own affairs has been honored by the succeeding Czars. Lately, the tide appears to have turned. The Bolsheviks are gaining enormous undeclared power, and their aim is to nationalize land through terrorism. Some of the more free thinkers among the settlers question the wisdom of the group staying so isolated and different. They feel if the first settlers had assimilated into the Russian culture, maybe now they would not be the target of so much hatred, distrust, and jealousy. They would not be so obviously different after all the generations have passed.

The settlers as a whole are a passive group, unconcerned with the outside world. They are content to live in their structured communities and mind their own business. Since the area is so large and their group is such an enormous contributor to the over all well being of the country, they feel things will continue on and this ill wind will soon pass. Little do they know, but a monster ideology has hatched and has been growing and multiplying just beyond their domain, an ideology that will soon consume and change their whole world forever.

The Bolsheviks are especially against the Czar and the ruling family. This, of course, makes Anton a prime target because until he came here and built this brewery, he had been the Austrian brewmaster for the Czar and his family. Czar Nicholas was good to Anton and his family and paid him well for his years of service. With the money he and Laura accumulated, they were able to come here to the Volga River Valley in Saratov and build this magnificent brewery; life should now be ideal. He and his family are back among their own people. He and Laura felt this would be especially important, so their three sons could find wives who shared their ethnic background. Now the new Trans-Siberian Railroad is almost complete and has opened many new and lucrative markets for the brewery. Sadly, with the growing political unrest and Laura's unexpected death, life is far from ideal for Anton.

This morning Anton really does not feel like discussing political issues with Alois because he has a worry he can't shake. His oldest son Joseph, the son most like Anton and the leader among the three sons, has told him three times about a young lady starting to attract his attention. Joseph, a very task-oriented young man, appears to be oblivious that he is being manipulated into spending time with her. She appears every where Joseph is, pretending it is a coincidence. Joseph has never had a girl pay attention to him before, and he is responding. Anton knows the girl's family, and he does not care for their way of living. While they are not exactly lazy, if the opportunity presents itself, they are forever trying to make a few dollars off of someone else's work.

Day before yesterday, Anton saw the young lady talking to Joseph, but they did not see him as he watched them. He could be mistaken, but he could almost see the dollar signs in the girl's eyes. She did not even try to disguise her efforts as she tried to attract his attention. This kind of openly aggressive behavior is so unlike the kind of refined lady he hopes Joseph will find. Since Joseph is the son he depends on the most, Anton feels Joseph needs a lady who will help polish the family's image.

He desperately wishes he had Laura here to talk to about this situation. They had been together so long and always discussed everything so openly. He can almost hear her agree with his observation. Didn't she always say that he's a good judge of character? He knows he needs to trust his own judgment, but what can he do to discourage Joseph away from the young lady? He and Laura always discussed how especially important it would be for Joseph to find a wife from their own kind. He also remembers how Laura had felt so strongly about this very kind of situation. She noticed many times when parents voiced opposition to a girlfriend, it had the opposite effect and actually drove the children toward the undesirable mate. This makes him reluctant to talk to Joseph about the problem.

As he lingers over his morning coffee, his thoughts drift back to his delightful little Martha as they did most mornings. If fate had not been so cruel and taken her away, she would be here to be the lady of the house. She would ease his pain over Laura's death and help Joseph find a suitable mate amongst her many girlfriends. Children should not die before their parents; it just isn't right, especially the death of his little Martha. She was such a loving happy child, their only daughter. As it has thousands of times before, his heart aches while he thinks about his little girl, who would be 18 years old now if only she had lived. His eyes wander to the last picture they had taken together. He and 10-year-old Martha had gone to Moscow to have the picture made at the Scherer Nabholzjiliez studio. The picture shows the bond of love between them. One of his hands holds her precious little fingers while the other holds her at the waist while she leans into him. He can still remember how she felt as they posed for that picture. They were both so happy with not a real care in the world. As he stares at the picture, he longs to go back to that time. He will never get to see her turn into a beautiful young lady. He will never walk her down the aisle on his arm, a vision of loveliness in a beautiful long gown with lots of family and friends gathered around. He will never get to enjoy being Grandfather to her babies. He has always thought he would enjoy being a good grandfather.

Lately he has felt so old, and although he never lets his boys know, some mornings he has a hard time getting out of bed. He is as tired in the morning as when he went to bed the night before. He wonders if he needs to slow down some, but he enjoys working with his boys. After all, isn't being surrounded by your family showing you how much they love you and respect your knowledge and ability one of the fruits of a long life?

His thoughts are interrupted by the sound of his two eldest sons as they come down the stairs. They are already discussing the day's work ahead of them in the brewery. Joseph looks so much happier than Anton has seen in years. He smiles as he talks to his brother and moves with a much easier step than usual. Joseph, unlike his two brothers, is a man of few words. He takes the responsibility of being the eldest son very seriously. Anton feels a slight twinge of guilt for the thoughts he has about the young lady who has brought this light-hearted air to his usually quiet son. The twinge soon passes when he thinks about how the eventual outcome of the situation will not be in Joseph's best interest (in his opinion).

Joseph returned home last month after graduating with honors from Brewmaster school at Frankfurt am Main in Germany. Anton knows his son probably knew more than some of the instructors when he left to go to school. He was almost disappointed when Joseph finished the school in record time. Anton had hoped he would spend some time looking for a wife, especially among the four daughters of the fine family where he boarded.

While in training, all Joseph could think about was his responsibilities as assistant brewmaster, and Joseph did not like being away from home. In the past, he had been on many business trips with his father, but that was different since they had a specific task to accomplish. When the business was complete, they had some fun with a few drinks and the best food they could find, and they came home again. He and his father are best of friends and really good business partners. His father always has a kind word about anything Joseph does, building his confidence daily. He loves working and pleasing his father.

When he left for school, things were different; his beloved mother had died just months before. He knew his father would carry the load of all the decisions made while he was gone to school. For the last 40 years, his parents had always depended on each other when making decisions. While his two brothers always do their part of the work, they are not really interested in the business end of making the beer.

The middle brother Georg, pronounced George, is a hard worker and is skilled in purchasing the supplies for the brewery. He can negotiate good buys on the raw products, but he hates the detail of paperwork and worrying about the overall running of the brewery. He is an excellent second-in-command. He can lead a large work force when he is told what needs to be done, but he dislikes calling the shots. After all, he has his dad and Joseph; they run things so well and make him feel so important. Why would he rock a really nice boat?

Father Anton Kara sits at the head of the barely adequate table in the cozy breakfast area off the kitchen in their otherwise large home. Laura liked to have the morning meal here in the smaller room even after the boys were gown and the room became a little cramped. She loved the effect of the beautiful sunshine as it came in the bay windows. She felt the light invigorated the spirit as it fell gently across the windowsill when it rose to dispel the darkness in the early morning hours. Breakfast was always eaten just as the sun came up. The young men around the table can remember only once when there was not a breakfast being served as the sun came up. It was on that dreadful day when Mama took sick in the middle of the night and died in the early morning hours.

Even though they had an excellent cook on staff, Mama was a hands-on lady. She loved to cook, especially breakfast, for "my four men" as she called them. She guarded this time as a private time for this small tight-knit family. The staff cleaned up after the meal was complete, so Laura could move on to her garden and the charity projects on her schedule for the day.

This morning, as the sun comes up outside the bay window, the light begins to reveal the beautiful array of Mama's roses blooming in profusion in the early morning mist. Once the garden was a source of lively conversation around the table, but now with Mama gone, it is still too soon to speak more than just a passing comment about the flowers. The rose garden had been Mama Laura's passion and another reason for having breakfast in this tiny nook. This was the only time her men really took time to look at and to enjoy her flower garden as the seasons came and went through the years. Their early morning enjoyment of her flowers and the beauty of the yard was her reward for her hard work and planning.

Mama Laura had at least one of every kind of rose she had ever heard of in her life. She kept two gardeners busy year round, but she did her part and dug in the dirt to grow her garden just like the hired hands. Together they tended the roses and an array of other flowers intertwined with small patches of lush green lawns. Many flowering ornamental trees surrounded the inner garden. People for miles around came to admire her garden and to seek advice on how to grow the plants. Laura even tried her hand at propagating some original rose varieties herself. The names and description of her beautiful accomplishments will be lost as history unfolds in the next years. The local Catholic Church as well as many charitable functions in the community had been benefactors of many beautiful arrangements of flowers from her garden.

In small plots scattered throughout the flower garden, she had an array of herbs for fresh use in the kitchen and throughout the house for fragrance. Near the long old abandoned coach house at the back of the property, she also had a huge vegetable garden to supply vegetables for her family and staff. The families of the men at the brewery shared the bounty of her green thumb.

As the all-male family finishes their breakfast, the young men leave to begin another long day at the brewery. Anton looks out the window and again thinks how he would love to have someone to talk to about his dilemma. He knows to whom he really wants to talk, but this morning, anyone with a discreet ear would do. Not a single person comes to mind. He is still lost in thought when the head gardener brings the household mail to him. Anton is delighted to see a letter from Laura's cousin Lela from Plzen, Austria.

Lela had always been Laura's favorite cousin, a kindred spirit in every way. In a small way, Anton feels his prayers have been answered. A letter from Lela is the next best thing to talking to Laura. Her letter is full of all kinds of information about the extended family back in Plzen and Prague, who died and who has married. In the latter paragraphs, she includes a little piece about a lady in Plzen. She is a rather well known lady, Amalia, the widow of the Baron Czerny to the Court of Austria. Anton remembers going to school with him years ago. The widow has been overtaken by grief after Baron Czerny's untimely accidental death. He had been on his way home from his duties as the overseer for all the properties of Franz Joseph when the buggy in which he was riding overturned. He died several days later from the massive head injuries.

Lela wrote that his widow had always enjoyed a little gambling on the side, but the baron had kept her in check. He allowed her a set amount of money, and when the money was gone, she had to stop. According to Lela's letter, his widow is now gambling away the family fortune at a rate sure to end in disaster. In fact, Lela mentioned the 19-year-old daughter of the couple had been invited to be a "Lady in Waiting in the court of Austria." However, now she will not be able to accept the honor because her mama has squandered the money she needs for the fine wardrobe and spending money. Lela goes on to say how the baron himself must be turning over in his grave as he was a very astute businessman. The daughter, his favorite child, could indeed have been a fine lady as she has a good head on her shoulders. She also mentions the daughter is beautiful, which he knows is not of paramount importance to Lela. It has always been their family's opinion that beauty is only skin deep. Anton can almost hear the old family adage told not only to give people a chuckle but also to give little boys a solid criterion to develop guidelines when they start looking for a wife. The story tells about an old mama and how she questions her son about his new girlfriend. She asks him if the young lady is strong, smart, frugal, and kind. Then she will ask if she is a good cook, if she loves children, and if she is friendly. After all those receive a positive reply, he is asked if she is pretty, the very least important attribute.

Anton Kara wastes no time in planning a trip to Plzen with Joseph in tow to check out this heaven-sent twist of fate. He is secretly wondering if Laura has reached across the great divide to provide this possible answer. Joseph isn't sure about this turn of events, but he has complete confidence his father has his best interest at heart.

Anton knows he isn't feeling as well as he used to, and he wants to give the running of the brewery over to Joseph. However, he wants to know what kind of wife his son will marry before he steps down. If she is a troublemaker or the like, it could spell trouble among the brothers, and he wants to guard against that if at all possible.

When the train arrives in Plzen, Anton and Joseph go to Lela's house. Anton has sent a telegram ahead, saying they would arrive around noon. He asked for Lela to please try to have an audience with the baron's widow arranged, if possible, for early afternoon.

Baroness Amalia Czerny receives the announcement and request with curious interest. She recognizes the name of Anton Kara, a local son who has done very well for himself. Through the years he and his family have seldom come back for visits. She is extremely curious as to why he wants to talk to her on this visit, so she arranges a time for Anton Kara to come to speak to her. With a few discreet inquiries, Amalia Czerny is able to ascertain and confirm that Anton Kara is no ordinary man. She already knows that for years he has been the brewmaster for Czar Nicholas of Russia. Now she learns that he has his own large brewery in the Volga River Valley in Saratov, Russia, and still makes the beer for the royalty of Russia. When she discovers the brewery is in an area full of beer-drinking German settlers, she thinks she has never heard of a more lucrative situation. She also gathers he has three unmarried sons, one old enough to be considered a bachelor. After some thought, Mama Amalia Czerny knows what she is going to do, but she tells no one.

Baroness Amalia Czerny had been from the court of Yugoslavia. Twenty years ago, she married the baron. During their long marriage, they lived the good life in Vienna. With the baron's prestigious position came many invitations to beautiful parties at the best places. They traveled all over the country to inspect the conditions of various properties and were wined and dined in the highest of fashion. Money was never a problem since Franz Joseph was generous to the baron for being as meticulous with the properties as if they were his own. He never allowed anyone to overcharge for services and required the utmost in quality services. The extra he paid the baron was easily made up and then some by the money he saved with his attention to details.

The Czernys have two separate families. The older children are from his first wife and are already married and on their own. One son is a successful professor at the University of Moravia, and the daughter is married to a prestigious lawyer in Prague. The other son has never found his place in the world and goes from job to job and woman to woman. Amalia is the mother of the two younger children still at home, one nineteen and the other only sixteen.

The baron inherited the family castle from his grandfather. The castle, which has been in the family for four generations, is a beautiful castle nestled on a small estate in Plzen, Austria, about 30 miles from Prague. The baron and his family enjoyed returning to the castle when they came home to visit their extended family. They kept a skeleton staff at the castle to keep everything in excellent shape. When they returned, they loved to entertain as often as time would allow. They had many friends and enjoyed a gracious life style.

After the baron's death, everything changed. The most obvious is he is no longer taking care of the family's business. Amalia had never taken care of anything; the baron felt that was his job and Amalia need not concern herself with business matters. The change that hurts the most is how the invitations to parties and social events have dried up like a prune into a raisin. Often Mama Amalia hears about parties old friends have given without inviting her, and it breaks her heart. Now the only social occasion available to her is gambling. At the casinos, no one seems to mind she is alone, not a half of a couple. For a few hours, she is special again. She has never been on her own and does not have a clue that the casino owners are just courting her money.

While the gambling started in innocence as she soothed her aching heart and found fun companionship, it is wreaking havoc with the family finances. She is sure everything will be all right. After all, the baron always said she should not worry her pretty little head about money. Her son-in-law tried to help her with her finances. At first, she welcomed his advice, but when he started to tell her she must stop gambling, she decided she never really liked him and broke off working with him on her finances. She knows there is an eminent danger she may already be in enough debt to lose the castle, but she has a new plan.

Anton Kara and Amalia Czerny meet on her downstairs veranda with an afternoon lunch set out like she is expecting royalty. Anton, like any normal person, loves the awe and respect Baroness Czerny is lavishing on her unsuspecting guest. She welcomes him into the family's home, an impressive castle. The furnishings are expensive, but he notices there are very few pieces of furniture. On the walls, there are many empty spaces where the paint is aged around where most likely a picture had been hanging. Also, in the entry hall, a very large rug is obviously missing. Logically, he knows these things should be of great concern, so he is wondering why alarms are not sounding in his head. Maybe the daughter will be just as shallow as the mother, but he trusts Lela's opinion that the daughter has a good head on her shoulders and is more like her father than her mother.

Meanwhile, Joseph tries to get a glimpse of the daughter Anna. After all, he wants to please his father, but if the courtship works out, he will be the one married to this woman. He wants to at least see what she looks like even if beauty is only skin deep. He questions Lela about the daughter and how he might get a chance to see her. Plzen is a relatively small town, so everyone always knows what everyone else is doing, especially if it is something they do on a regular schedule. She tells him that at this time of day, young Anna will be at dance lessons with a local teacher. Lela accompanies him to point Anna out. They wait across the street from the studio in a little coffee shop, and soon she comes out with a young man and a group of other students from the class. Oh yes! He sees she is a really nice (beautiful) young woman. She appears to know everyone she meets on the street. He is more than impressed; his heart likes what he sees. He does not understand the strange sensation he is feeling, but he sure derives pleasure from looking at this beautiful young Anna Czerny.

He finds his reaction to the young lady to be ever so delightful, but now he knows he has a real problem. He has never been any good with women, maybe one date and that was the end. Now, how will he impress this exquisite beauty he wants with all his heart and soul? The thought crosses his mind that he would have been better off if he had never seen her. He knows he has confidence in abundance when he conducts business and when he invests money, but when it comes to women, he has always been a complete failure. Thinking back, he realizes he never was as interested in any female like he is interested in this stunning creature. He convinces himself that genuinely wanting the woman will help him come across with more confidence. (He hopes!) He also hopes his father Anton and Anna's mother have gotten along well and have made plans, so he can begin courting this lovely person. He realizes he has never wanted anything more in his entire life. He is amazed at how he feels. An hour ago, he was a rational, content man with a full life, a life that met all his needs. Now he doesn't know how he feels, but for some reason, he knows he will never be quite the same again.

Joseph and his father are scheduled to meet back at Cousin Lela's house about mid-afternoon. Joseph can tell his father is upset the minute he sees him. His heart sinks, and all kinds of possibilities run through his head. Joseph finds himself almost holding his breath in anticipation of finding out why his father is upset. Never in a million years would he have guessed the problem.

Anton is impressed with the mother, who is so gracious and refined. However, the bottom line of their little meeting is the woman asked for a large sum of money for her daughter to marry his son. Anton knows buying a wife has been an accepted practice for centuries in many cultures, but he feels it is such a cold way to get a wife. He is inclined to just get back on the train and leave without so much as a word to the uppity woman, who had the audacity to offer her daughter for sale here at the dawn of the twentieth century.

However, Anton, forever the logical businessman who is not inclined to snap decisions, makes arrangements with Mama Czerny for another meeting in an hour after he has a chance to talk to Joseph. Anton expects Joseph to say the idea of buying a bride is totally out of the question. When Joseph doesn't nix the idea and is actually interested in his father working on the negotiations, Anton's whole perception of the situation changes. Joseph confides in his father that he has had a glimpse of the young lady and really liked what he saw. Anton begins to understand the desirability of this proposed arrangement. He also knows his son is not likely to sweep a young, spirited woman off her feet at first sight, and at best, a long courtship will be difficult because of the distance. Anton needs Joseph back in Saratov but sees from the urgency in Joseph's mannerisms and comments that he might even decide to stay here if necessary to win his young lady's affection. Within the hour, both parents meet again. A deal for an undisclosed large sum of money is agreed upon. (The parents never disclose the sum, but they both agreed it was a lot.)

Fortunately, that very evening there is a social planned at the Catholic Church in Plzen, the one the Czerny family and Kara ancestors have belonged to for generations. Both young

Anna and Joseph go to the occasion. Joseph is accompanied by Lela's youngest son Heinrich. They start out at separate ends of the large party room, but as the evening progresses, Joseph slowly works his way to the other side of the room where Anna is visiting with her friends.

All afternoon he has rehearsed the interesting things he will say to introduce himself to Anna. When he gets to where she stands, he introduces himself. In the second sentence, he asks her to marry him. Her mother had told Anna she had to accept, so she accepts his proposal right there on the spot. They dance away the rest of the evening, getting to know and to like each other, or so Joseph thinks.

All the Czerny family and friends and the Kara relations still living close at hand in Prague come at short notice for a big engagement party and stay for the wedding the next day. The scenario in a nutshell: one day they meet, the next day they have an engagement party, the third day they marry. Late on the third day, Joseph and Anna leave on a honeymoon, still almost complete strangers. Two months earlier, Anna had planned on being a "Lady in Waiting to the Court in Austria" with all its glamour and possibilities of living happily ever after, but now she finds herself married to a man she hardly knows. Young Anna is nineteen years old, and Joseph is twenty-nine years old. He is not much fun, not like her young dance class partner she has been flirting with for years. She cannot believe she is married to such a boring man.

Anton Kara leaves almost immediately after the service to return to the brewery since both he and Joseph have been gone a lot longer than they had planned. The thought might have occurred to him that he needed to get out while the getting is good, before Mama Czerny decides she needs a rich man to marry. She does have a winning way about her, but he also needs to return as quickly as possible to be sure the different stages of fermentation in progress for the beer is being monitored closely enough. Georg can be trusted to do what is expected, but if anything unexpected or complicated arises as it usually does, he might not be able to handle it easily since he has little actual brewmaster experience. Not because he cannot learn the process, but because he never needed to since Anton and Joseph always take care of everything.

Anton buys a first class train trip for the couple to have a leisurely return trip to the brewery. Anna and the household staff have to get all her belongings packed and on the train several hours after the reception, which is no small task for a young woman who has a passion for beautiful expensive glass and art and has already amassed a large collection. Her treasures are packed with such care and concern by the family's few remaining well-trained staff. If she had a crystal ball to look into the future, she would have left her precious things at home, but no, that was not a desirable option either because Mama would lose them gambling. With all her belongings safely loaded on the train, the young couple waves "goodbye" to family and friends as they embark on their life together.

Joseph behaves like the gentleman his mother and father raised; he puts no demands on his new wife even though as a bought wife she has absolutely no rights left under the laws and morés of the times. One would have to wonder how Mama Amalia Czerny could subject her beloved daughter, her late husband's pride and joy, to the possibility of such disrespectful treatment. Apparently, the thought has not occurred to Anna either.

The newlyweds eat the evening meal in the dining car on the train and then retire to their sleeper for the evening. It isn't long before naïve, unsuspecting Joseph falls sound asleep. By this time, reality settles in on Anna, and she panics. When the train stops at the next stop, she gets off to go back home to Mama with no money and no idea how to get home.

When Joseph wakes up, he discovers his new bride is gone. He and the crew search the entire train and find she is not even on the train. Being a realistic man, he knows the dangers his young wife can encounter. She is out there somewhere alone without any money, and he is terrified for her safety. At the next stop, he sends a telegram back to Mama Czerny. He tells her what has happened and he will wait here at the station for Anna to return. Mama Czerny gets some of her kinfolks, and they start a search. They find Anna, disoriented and scared, sitting at the station where she got off the train. They take her back to Joseph. Sadly, in the short time between when Joseph and Anna left Plzen and when she got the telegram, Mama Czerny has already gambled away a big hunk of the money she received from the sale of her daughter. Even if she wants to, she cannot help her daughter get out of this marriage arrangement.

Mama has a long talk with Anna on the way back to meet Joseph. She tells her she is married to this man and there is no way out of the situation. She needs to make the best of the situation; after all, the Karas are wealthy, which is all that matters to Mama Czerny. Young Anna thinks her mama is the smartest woman and trusts her opinion completely, so she decides not to run away again. Actually, she had been more frightened than she has ever been in her life when she was in that train station with no family and no money. Now, Mama Czerny confesses to Anna that she is about to lose their home, the castle. Young Anna begins to understand as never before how her life in Plzen as she knew it is over. The shame and disgrace of being poor in a small city where she has always been wealthy would be more than she wants to experience, so she begins to realize the marriage to Joseph is a golden opportunity.

Joseph gets his young bride back in a much more contrite and cooperative frame of mind. To the end of his days, Joseph is eternally grateful to Mama Czerny for returning his beloved Anna to him with such an improved attitude. He never sees it is a selfish act on her part since he has never had any dealings with manipulative women. Throughout their lives, he never looks for ulterior motives in Mama and Anna. He always treats them like they are treasures he is privileged to have in his life. As their time on the honeymoon progresses, Anna starts to relax and even kind of like Joseph. He is such a good man, like her father, and she begins to see his good qualities.

Chapter 2

When Joseph and his bride arrive in Saratov, Papa Anton meets them at the train. He takes them to their beautiful mansion to meet the brothers. The two brothers, along with the family staff, greet them at the front steps. The house is not as big as Anna's castle in Plzen, but it is a beautiful home with splendid grounds. It looks like a warm and comfortable place to live. Anna knows she can have a good life here.

Shortly after she is introduced to the brothers, Papa Anton presents Anna with a welcome gift, changing her mind about the whole deal. He presents Anna with her very own beautiful new carriage with matching horses with a driver at her disposal. He tells her to go into town and buy what ever she wants. Now she knows he is a man after her own heart! The warm welcome and the gesture of the fabulous gift set the stage for how she will live her life. She buys what she wants when she wants it, no expense spared. Thankfully, she has more intelligence than her mother and does not buy her way into the poor house. Evidently, she has some of her father's logical traits.

Anna loves her new life as the lady of a beautiful home with four handsome men, who give her lots of attention. Anton is so proud of his accomplishment he can hardly keep from bragging. He loves Anna, who loves to host parties, and her parties are second to none, which is a real plus for the brewery and its public image. She never considers doing any of the actual work around the house and yard like his beloved Laura, but since they have made a lot of money with the brewery, he can afford to indulge this gracious and beautiful lady. With the completion of some of the Trans-Siberian Railroad, many new markets have opened, markets previously inaccessible, and the entire route will soon be complete, which will give the brewery a bigger market, more customers, and an increase in profits.

After several months, Anton asks the staff to prepare a party just for the family. He tells the family it is a celebration to welcome Anna, but he actually has a bigger plan in mind. After the evening meal, he announces he is going to retire. He announces Joseph, the oldest, will be the brewmaster while Georg will be in charge of purchasing and Alois will be in charge of sales. Joseph is so honored he can hardly keep the buttons on his shirt from popping off. The two other brothers are also pleased as neither one wants the responsibility of being brewmaster and both have known all their lives Joseph would be the next brewmaster. Anna is lukewarm about the whole idea because she knows it will require longer hours for Joseph. She has begun to enjoy Joseph's company and attention. She likes things like they are, but when she sees how proud Joseph is, she changes her attitude and thanks Papa Anton with genuine enthusiasm. She realizes for the first time that she has learned to love this fine man, her new husband, for what he can give her but mostly for the way he looks at her. She actually feels a desire to please Joseph.

They had planned to wait a while before they would tell the family, but Joseph whispers to Anna and gets her consent to return father's benevolence with an announcement of their own. With boisterousness and cantor Joseph seldom displays, he exclaims, "We are having a baby, the first Kara heir!" What a wonderful evening for the Anton Kara family! They are all so excited about the baby, but Alois is really excited because he loves children, especially little babies.

The following morning, Joseph assumes his new position. He is bound and determined to make his father proud of him. He relishes the great responsibility and honor his father has bestowed on him by entrusting him with his life's work. Joseph has a few ideas how he can do things a little better, but for now, he will carry on exactly as before to be sure his father does not have any cause to regret his decision. After all, Father has placed such great trust in him with a position usually held by much older more mature men.

Anton Kara throws himself into being retired. After about a week of it, he has done everything he wanted to do. He tries to keep himself busy, especially in Laura's flower garden, but everything there just brings back memories of his lost love. The head gardener and his crew have taken up all the slack left when Laura died. When Anton feels useless, he doesn't do well. He has felt poorly for a long time, but with things to do, he could function. Since retirement, he feels like he is falling apart. He used to enjoy visiting with his friends at the taverns in town or here at the brewery's tasting room; however, now, the conversations always turn to the Bolsheviks and how they are gaining power. He does not like what is going on and feels he is powerless to stop what he knows needs to be stopped. Within six months, Antonius Joseph Kara is dead at the age of 70 years and two months. In reality, his death is a blessing; if he had lived a few more years, he would have seen heart-wrenching changes in the Volga River Valley and unthinkable things perpetrated on his beloved family and business. It would have killed his soul if he had been alive.

Joseph and Anna get the message from Marie that Mama has indeed lost the castle and they are now homeless and destitute. Marie has a job, but Mama has no skills and is reluctant to look for a job, which she feels is below her social status. Joseph and Anna discuss the situation, and Joseph offers to purchase a boarding house in Prague for her mother and Marie. It will stay in Joseph's name, and he will hire a person from the bank in Prague to oversee the situation so it will be a secure source of income. They purchase the apartments in Prague, so Marie and Mama will no longer be in Plzen.

The family falls into a comfortable routine in the household. Anton and Laura are gone, and Joseph and Anna are now the head of the family, which is all right with the brothers. They like Anna, especially Alois, and her parties are the talk of the town. Now he can really impress the young women, and impress them he does! At the mention of some young woman's name, there is no Father Anton around to scrawl his face because he thinks she is not good enough for his son. As Alois intends never to marry, what is the difference anyway? Why would he tie himself down to one woman when he can have so many? Joseph and Anna can have the children to continue the Kara line, and he will help spoil them. Life is good on the home front, but all too often there are reports of the Bolsheviks with the Communist movement harassing some of the German settlers on the fringe of the valley. Maybe those settlers did something they should not have done, or at least the Kara men used that rationale to ease their worries about the growing threat of the Communist ideology.

When Alois is in town at the taverns and whenever people gather together, he always has to speak his peace. Georg is not very articulate, but when he is there, he is drawn into the conversations and expresses his opinion, also. Joseph is at home with his responsibilities at the brewery and his expectant wife, so he is seldom involved in the debates.

Times are getting harder, and reports of settlers being killed now come often from all over the valley. The locals can no longer rationalize away the brutality and hatred being reported. As they do not have any official form of government, they have no way to protest the injustices being perpetrated on the innocent settlers. They know the root cause of the problem is the fact that these Communists want their land now that they have made it productive and the Czar is losing power. The Bolsheviks spout theories that land needs to be owned by everyone and no one has the right to own land individually. Alois has a real hard time keeping his mouth shut and sometimes doesn't.

Amidst all the brewing turmoil, Georg meets a young woman at a friend's house. Regina is Russian, a raving beauty with coal black hair and piercing black eyes. She has a light heartedness Georg loves, somewhat uncharacteristic of many Russian women. She is fun to be with, like the women his brother Alois always has around him, but she is a woman of high standards and respected by everyone. Reminiscent of how Joseph had fallen in love with Anna in Plzen, Georg falls in love, head over heels in love. To Georg's elation, there is one huge difference--Regina returns his overtures of affection immediately.

Georg and Regina both love to dance and to spend many hours at the local festivals. They dance every dance, lost in their own world. They need only to be together to be absolutely happy. It isn't long before Georg takes her home to meet his family.

He knows if his father Anton had still been alive, he would have looked at the situation with very skeptical eyes since the girl is not of German or Czech heritage. Joseph is now filling Anton's shoes. Georg knows, out of the respect the three brothers have always had for each other, that Joseph will not actually challenge his choice for a wife. True to form, Joseph broaches the subject only to be sure Georg has considered the difference in their families but then drops the subject and never mentions it again. He feels Georg is a grown man and his selection of a companion for life has to be his choice. He can see how happy Regina has made his brother.

Anna's reaction to Regina is another story; she was raised to believe people should marry only people of their own nationality. Anna intends to give Regina a cold shoulder when she comes to visit the first time in hopes that maybe she will disappear. When Anna gives a cold shoulder, a person can freeze to death in a heat wave. Georg and Regina (and everyone else) clearly get the message of Anna's dislike for Regina. For the first time in his married life, Joseph puts his foot down and stops the problem right then and there. He takes his wife aside and tells her in no uncertain terms that her behavior is totally unacceptable. This house they enjoy so much is as much Georg's home as theirs. If this is the woman with whom Georg wants to spend his time, she is to be treated with respect and kindness, and nothing less will be acceptable.

Never before has Joseph talked to her with such resolve and confidence. Anna usually knows how to play him like a violin, but this time she knows it is time to do what he asks without trying to change his mind to get her way. She can remember only once when her father, the baron, talked to her in such a stern manner. When he did, she learned he meant business and to do contrary to his wishes earned severe results. In fact, she realizes there are a lot of parallels in this situation. As a child, her father found her being just horrible to the butler's little girl. The baron usually spoke gently when he talked to Anna, but this day he laid down the law in no uncertain terms and expected her to change her behavior. This rudeness would not be allowed in his house. His staff worked hard, and they and their families deserved respect.

Anna can still remember how she was momentarily deterred but naively decided that her beloved father could not have meant what he had said. She convinced herself he had just said it for the benefit of the staff that was present. The next opportunity she got the girl alone, she again harassed the child more unmercifully than before. Much to her surprise, she realized her father had deliberately monitored her actions.

He took her aside into his study, and not even her mother was allowed to enter while they settled the issue. He took out a paddle and put her across his knee. He told her he had made himself very clear before, and she had not understood or believed him enough to obey his orders. He wanted to know if she understood how things were to be done in his house. She knew from the look in his eye that he meant every word he said, and she resolved to never push him to that point again.

Now Joseph has a similar look in his eye. Her usually gentle husband feels very strongly on this issue, and she can see he is not going to accept anything less than her cooperation. She decides to play her cards in a different fashion. She begins to weep and tells Joseph she is so sorry. She will apologize to Georg and Regina and make every effort to welcome Regina in the future. Joseph is visibly pleased with her change of heart. She apologizes and begins treating Regina as a special guest. In her heart, she plans to never like Regina out of spite for this situation.

Regina's parents are fairly well off. Her father is a construction supervisor with the new Trans-Siberian Railroad, which is reaching completion, so her entire family will soon be moving out of the region. Regina's parents and Georg get along very well. However, while her father doesn't actually belong to the Communist movement in the area, he is somewhat sympathetic to their overall concept. Georg worries that their differing political views may hinder his relationship with Regina.

Regina's mother is not in agreement with the Communist movement. She can see the people in leadership are ruthless men with no regard for people. She can also see they are just mean men pushing their ideas, no matter who gets hurt. Regina often hears her father and mother discussing the individual Red leaders, especially Igor Ivanson, the man her father spends the most time with. Her mother feels he is an especially mean and hateful man. She has heard how, for no reason, he turned on people who trusted him. Until her dying day, Regina regrets not taking heed and believing the words of warning her mother spoke about this wicked man.

Georg and Regina set their wedding day and discuss the plans for their reception. They spend lots of time at the Kara house, and while Anna may not like the young woman, she cannot resist the opportunity to throw a wedding reception. However, her time to deliver the child is at hand, and she is unable to take charge of everything. Regina is relieved; after all, it is her wedding. She welcomes Anna's suggestions, but she wants to make the final decisions with Georg.

After the evening meal on Sunday, Anna feels exceptionally tired and goes up to bed early. Joseph, Georg, and Regina are still seated around the table when the upstairs maid comes in all wide-eyed and flustered. She tells Joseph that Anna has asked for both he and Regina to come up to her bedroom. When they get up to the bedroom, they find Anna in a state of confusion. There is bloody water all over the bed, and a little head is already showing between her legs.

Regina is the oldest child in a family of eight children, so she has assisted with many of her mother's births. She is amazed at how far the birth has already progressed in such short time. What really surprises her is that Anna has not cried out once in pain and appears not to have any pain as the head comes through the birth canal. She remembers some of the older women in her family talking about a woman who did not have labor pains, but none of them had actually believed it could happen. Every birth Regina had witnessed was like the woman was in a torture chamber with no relief in sight. In fact, during one birth, the dogs outside the house began to howl in response to the mother's screams.

Regina takes charge and sends the maid downstairs to get warm water in a big pan and lots of clean sheets. Almost before the maid gets out of the door, the baby slips out onto the bed. Things are happening so fast that Regina does not know what to do next. She reaches for the baby and picks up the bloody squirming screaming little creature just in time to lift it above the after birth, which comes out with a gush. As quickly as it started, the birth is over. Completely!

When they all realize what has just happened, they start to laugh, a little at first and then more and more. They cannot believe what has just occurred. Joseph and Georg are not experienced with the usual length of a birth experience, but they know it is supposed to be a long and painful one. Regina and some of the house staff are experienced and know it was nothing short of a miracle. What a joyous occasion! In all the excitement, they have not focused on the baby. Anna is the first to exclaim, "Oh! Look! My baby is a little *girl*! Isn't she just beautiful? Here give her to me; I want to hold her." Regina places the little girl in her mother's arms. Anna coos and hums to the infant as the child squirms in her arms. Joseph sits on the bed and beholds the beautiful sight. He is a happy man, Anna is a happy mama, and they have a beautiful healthy little angel. What a beautiful scene!

A nurse is brought in to take care of the baby's every need, so all Anna has to do is play with her little girl, named Heidwecka Anna Kara, Hettie for short. From the night of Hettie's birth, the relationship between Regina and Anna changes completely. Anna loves to have Regina around since she knows so much about babies. Anna takes Regina's advice as if she is her mother.

With a painless birth and a nurse to care for the baby, Anna is soon back up to par, ready to plan the wedding with new zest and vigor. Since she now has a new respect for Regina, Anna works hard to be sure she is pleased with every aspect of the plan. They work together like loving sisters. They giggle and laugh as they find out they both have a lot of the same tastes. Regina no longer resents Anna's involvement and feels it is all done with her best interest at heart. Georg and Joseph just get out of the way and slap each other on the back in elation as they enjoy seeing their women getting along so well after such a rough start. Never has the house been so full of life and enjoyment

True to form, the wedding is a beautiful affair. There are six bridesmaids and six groomsmen. Regina did not know which sister to pick as maid of honor, so she settled the problem by asking Anna to be her matron of honor with her five sisters as the other bridesmaids. Joseph is his brother's best man. Alois is the first groomsman, and Georg's friends from college are the other four groomsmen. Regina's niece and nephew are the junior bridesmaid and groomsman. Regina's two-year-old twin brother and sister stole the show as ring bearer and flower girl.

The bridesmaids' dresses are a beautiful canary yellow with lace and ribbon in abundance, both on the sweet heart neckline and down the skirt. Regina's dress is a beautiful white lace creation designed by Rosa, a local seamstress. The dress she makes is a labor of love for the bride of Laura's son. She had sewn for Laura Kara for years, and Laura had always made sewing for her such a pleasure. About five years earlier, Laura helped Rosa and her family out when they had a fire in their house. The fire did not destroy a lot, but the smut and stink took weeks to clean out of everything. Laura invited the family to stay at her guesthouse at the brewery. Laura had her staff look after the little ones during the day, so Rosa could work without interruption. Laura brought food for the friends helping Rosa's family clean up, and she stayed to help clean for three long days.

The fire started in the kitchen, next to Rosa's sewing area, so all the dresses she was working on at the time of the fire were ruined. Laura was appalled so many of the well-to-do ladies expected Rosa to replace their material and notions destroyed in the fire. Laura went to the merchant Mr. Lehmann at the dry goods store and persuaded him to sell the material and notions to Rosa for a fraction of the usual price. Rosa suspected Laura had slipped Mr. Lehmann some money to defray his loss, but maybe not since Mr. Lehmann told Rosa that Laura had told him the reason he got to sell so much material was because Rosa sewed so beautifully and quickly. Laura thought he should help Rosa out in her time of need. When asked about it, she answered, "It is just the right thing to do."

Regina is resplendent in her wedding dress. Her black hair is piled high on her head with a few ringlets to soften the effect, framing her exquisite oval shaped face and accentuating her dark eyes. Georg cannot take his eyes off of his beautiful bride.

Georg and Regina take a short wedding trip. Upon their return, life again falls into a regular routine. Regina likes to cook, and the men are elated when she decides to cook breakfast every morning, "just like Mama." At first the food is not as good as the cook had served, and they each silently wonder if this is a good idea. Steadily, the food improves, and they love the time together without staff. Joseph has taken an active interest in the roses in the flower garden just outside the bay windows of the breakfast area, so again the conversation around the breakfast table often revolves around the flowers in the morning mist.

The Kara men are not in agreement with Czar Nicholas's policies. He has surrounded himself with such bad advisors, and every decision he is making lately helps his opposition. When Germany declares war on France, Russia comes into the war on France's side. Now the Germans in the valley are being viewed as enemies even though they have been in Russia for generations and are loyal Russian citizens. The men try to downplay the terrible unrest in the valley, but people, too scared to remain, have started to leave the valley. There are so many factions and ideologies vying for power in Russia. The Red Russians, as they like to be called, are the largest faction, but others are gaining strength. Many of them often intimidate the settlers, and occasionally they carry out their threats so the people will get scared. And scared they are because dissenters seem to be everywhere. They are sneaky and have so little respect for the rights of the settlers. They step over lines of accepted behavior and eavesdrop on conversations when others would feel ashamed to listen. The settlers feel uneasy whenever they talk with anyone because they never know who is eavesdropping, who is sympathetic to the Communist cause, or who simply hates Germans.

Alois' love of debate has led to many confrontations with the Reds, and he is finally aware that they do not take his banter as just debate for fun. More and more, he is keeping himself to groups clearly sharing his view; however, he has already made a name for himself, which he regrets. As salesman for the brewery, he occasionally has to be in contact with people with strong dissenting opinions. They invariably provoke him into conversations he knows he should avoid. Georg tries to keep his distance from Alois when they are out on business, but they are brothers. When Alois is unfairly cornered, Georg invariably comes to his defense.

Before long, Regina and Georg announce she is pregnant. The entire household is ecstatic, and the new baby will be born soon enough to be a good playmate to Hettie. They all enjoy Hettie. Many evenings the sitting room is filled with laughter as they watch little Hettie learn new things. First she rolls over and begins to crawl at an early age. She appears to be a child of above average intelligence, but they aren't sure since they know they might be a little biased when it comes to Hettie. For such a young age, she is an exceptionally agile, happy, and easy child.

Regina soon becomes unable to function because she is always sick. In the morning, she can no longer prepare breakfast without many trips to the drain in the kitchen to throw up. The cook offers to once again prepare the morning meal, and Regina does not object. Without breakfast to prepare, she stays in her room until midmorning. This is better; she does not have to smell food. However, she is so tired that she returns to the bedroom before noon each day for another nap, so uncharacteristic of Regina. She seldom takes naps and really does not think much of people who take naps. Just before their first anniversary and before the first trimester of her pregnancy passes, Regina starts to spot. The doctor confines her to bed. Even that does not help, and soon she realizes that no matter what she does, the pregnancy is going to end. Her pain when she loses the baby is as much as some women have in a real birth. Anna is there to help her through her difficulty and tries to ease her pain as much as possible with hot packs and rubs. Anna realizes how fortunate she had been when Hettie was born; in fact, she is over whelmed while helping Regina. She has never been around when anyone had a baby, so she really has no idea what she had missed. Now she has a much clearer idea.

Eventually the physical pain stops, but Regina is crushed. She so wanted a baby like Hettie, and now the sight of Hettie is painful. Everyone tells her that she is young and will have other babies, but for Regina, it isn't that simple to forget about the life that never will be lived. Anna also appears to be in mourning along with Regina. They have gotten so close that Regina's pain is Anna's pain. The house is not a happy place, but slowly things return to normal. Eventually, Regina returns to making breakfast each morning as the sun lightens the horizon.

Hettie begins walking at eleven months old and now is always into something. She is becoming quite a ham, and she enjoys the attention of so many adults. Alois loves to play the harmonica in the evening while Hettie dances for the enjoyment of all, family and staff alike. Joseph loves to take her into the rose garden in the afternoon when he takes his break from the brewery. She plays in the grassy area with the kittens living under the nearby gardener's shed. Anna and Regina play a simple version of hide and seek with Hettie to hear her screech when they jump out of hiding. Life in the Kara house is good again.

When Hettie is a little over a year old, Anna discovers she is pregnant again. She dreads telling Regina as Regina is becoming concerned since she is not getting pregnant again. (She feels surely enough time has passed.) Anna only tells Joseph, but it isn't long before Regina notices Anna is getting thicker through the middle. Finally, she confronts Anna with her suspicions and chastises Anna severely for not telling her sooner. True to her nature, Regina is as excited about the coming child as if it were her own. Anna begins to realize she is showing this pregnancy much earlier than she did with Hettie, but she dismisses her observation.

When the baby starts to move, it is like a tug of war in her womb. Other people, especially the older women, start to notice Anna is a lot bigger than she should be for her time. They suggest either she is carrying twins or she is much farther along than she had figured.

Meanwhile, things with the Bolsheviks have gotten much worse. Droves of the settlers all over the valley are leaving to move farther inland toward Siberia, where they hope to start a new life in safety. As they leave, the Red Communists gain more and more power and push harder and harder. Their plan is to take the settlers' land and then assign people to produce the crops and to share the produce and income from the land. There will be no private land, just land owned by the government they are going to set up when they get rid of the Czar and his régime.

The ominous situation is no longer something the Kara men can rationalize away. They know it is just a matter of time until the Communists come to take over the brewery, which affects Joseph more than the other two brothers. Father entrusted the brewery (his life's work) into Joseph's hands, and now he can do nothing to stop this monstrous thing biting at his heels. The brothers know things are especially bad for the brewery because the Communist Regime is especially against any kind of alcohol. They claim the consumption of alcohol makes people non-productive. This concept is especially asinine to the Karas and the Germans in the valley. They have always enjoyed their beer and wine and have turned the valley into one of the most productive areas of Russia or the world for that matter.

One sunny day, Regina and Anna come out on the veranda to rest for a little while with a cup of coffee. Anna feels something start to run down her leg. When she looks, she discovers her water has broken. Almost at the same time as she realizes what is happening, she begins to feel the baby coming out. Anna hurries to the day bed along the wall of the veranda and lies down. As she does, the baby's head is already almost half out. Regina is caught off guard for a moment and stands there with her mouth open. When she realizes what is happening, she calls for the staff to get water and blankets. Out comes the most beautiful little boy she has ever seen. From experience, she reaches for the infant to pick him up, so he will not be drowned in the after birth she expects to come whooshing out any minute. But, the after birth does not come. Regina screeches with excitement; there is another head coming out. Anna is in a state of confusion, but when she hears Regina screech, she wants to know what is wrong. Regina can barely believe Anna is actually having no pain and does not realize she is having another baby. Regina tells Anna there is another baby coming out, and Regina hands the first baby to Joseph, who has appeared out of nowhere. She reaches for the second baby, another boy, to lift him above the after birth if it comes this time. The afterbirth comes out with a whoosh. In a matter of minutes, the birth of twins is over! Completely!

Anna feels normal almost immediately. She wants to hold her little boys and holds out both arms with a huge smile on her face. Regina places the second born in her arm on one side as Anna kisses his cheek and hugs him. Joseph puts the firstborn son in her other arm. They planned to name a son Maximilian Anton Kara, but now they have to select another name for the second son. They name him Hans Anton Kara. Since the twins are identical, they knit little caps to tell them apart. They are beautiful blond, blue-eyed, healthy little boys. Joseph is overjoyed. Not only does he have a son to carry on the Kara name and become the brewmaster, now he has two. He has been blessed indeed.

The household is overjoyed with the little boys, but the political scene has become a point of terror. Daily, people are forced from their homes, and if they refuse, the father, the head of the household, is shot on the spot in front of his family, and sometimes the whole family is killed without provocation.

The brothers prepare an escape plan for the whole family. They have to get the supplies and food together without the knowledge of the workers in the brewery and some of the house staff as now-a-days they can trust almost no one. They will load two wagons and a carriage and head out toward Siberia. They know heading toward China is their only chance of escape because everyone will be looking for them toward Prague and Europe since they have family there. They also know there is turmoil all over Europe, and they will not be welcomed even if they can get back to Prague. Here in Russia, they are considered enemies of the government because they are German. If they try to return to Austria at this time, they will be considered enemies of Austria because they are from Russia. Austria and Hungary are in an alliance against a coalition of countries with Russia and her allies.

Joseph plans the escape as meticulously as he does everything else, down to the last detail. He knows they need to travel lightly, but they need to have supplies for the long trip. He also knows if the family dares to take their fancy carriage, they will stand out like a sore thumb in the countryside. He asks one of his trusted servants to bring as simple a carriage as he can find, one that looks old but is in good repair. He also plans to use several of the wagons from the brewery. The brothers, along with four servants they trust implicitly, help gather the things and prepare them for the trip. They make sure they have their rifles and buy as much ammunition as they can gather without attracting attention. They know they might need them for protection, but they will also need them to shoot game on the trip. A few wagon repair parts, pots and pans, a tent, seasonings, soap-- so much to think of when a family with little children is going to be on the road so long with the Siberian winter approaching. Joseph packs a chest with Russian rubles (paper money) so that they can buy things along the way, but they know the route they plan to travel will have few if any people, especially when they get farther into Siberia. They know they will need money to start a new life when they get to Harbin, China, their planned destination. Joseph has Regina sew Anna's jewels in the lining of their winter coats. He folds them in the trunk on the back of the carriage. He knows that, if necessary, they can be used as money when they get to their destination. It also helps assure Anna she will not have to leave all of her prized possessions behind.

This morning they are so glad they have always had breakfast alone. They can finalize their plans without arousing any suspicions. Anna is thankful Regina will be along since she can help her take care of the children and calm her fears. Three of their trusted servants have agreed to accompany them as far as the Chinese border. When they get that far, the servants will return to Saratov with one wagon, which by then, will be enough to carry their remaining supplies. The family also agrees that if for some reason they get separated, as well they might, they will contact Cousin Lela in Prague. She will be the only one they all know who will not be watched to discover their whereabouts.

They plan to leave this evening after it gets dark, so they will be able to get a long way from the brewery before they are missed. Everything is planned, and they try to appear as normal as possible as they go about their usual tasks. Georg and Alois go on to the brewery while Joseph goes to put several items in the carriage, which is hidden in the old carriage house at the back of their property.

As he walks back into the house, he is met in the front hall by his bookkeeper, who is as white as a sheet. He tells Joseph the Bolsheviks just stormed into the brewery, arrested Georg and Alois at gunpoint, and took them off to be put into prison! He said they also looked for Joseph and will come back for him later. Regina comes into the room as the clerk is telling Joseph, screams at the top of her lungs, and begins to wail. With terror in her eyes through her sobs, she wants to know the names of the men who arrested Georg. When the clerk tells her it was Igor Ivanson, a flash of hope brushes her expression and then disappears. With great sobs, she tells Joseph and the clerk that she knows the man. He is a man her father did business with in the past. As she thinks about it, she also remembers her mother thought him to be a ruthless man with no compassion or scruples. She keeps that thought to herself and tells Joseph her father considered him a friend. That was true three years ago, but she doesn't know now if Igor Ivanson is a friend or foe.

Joseph wants so badly to try to help his brothers, but he knows it would be suicide. He understands he has to be alive to protect and to provide for his three children. If he goes to prison or dies, they will be at the mercy of every horrible element in this dreadful world in which they now live.

He knows it is a calculated risk, but he figures the Bolsheviks will not expect for him to be loaded and ready to go. The wagons he has packed are beer delivery wagons, which leave the brewery everyday. By this time, Anna has heard the commotion and is in the room trying to console Regina, who tells her through sobs what has happened. Except for Chang, the children's nurse, they dismiss all the household staff from the house, and they go into Joseph and Anna's bedroom. Joseph tells them they will have to be ready to leave in one hour, the usual time the delivery wagons always leave the brewery.

With absolute resolution, Regina tells them she will not leave without Georg. She has to stay and try to get him out of prison. She is his only hope, and she will not desert her husband in his hour of need. She tells them she is Russian, so she will be all right and will be able to get along by herself until she can get Georg out of prison. They will follow and catch up with them. Joseph and Anna know they will never change her mind, for they have witnessed the depth of her love for Georg. Joseph quickly puts on the clothes he has gotten from the head gardener to wear so that he will blend in when they get out in the countryside. He embraces Regina, and for just a moment, they both cry in each other's arms and kiss each other on the cheek.

Joseph tells Regina where there is money in the study that she can use. She will be the only person left in the house. Joseph tells Anna to get the children ready. He knows he needs to get out of the house and be undercover until they leave. He knows at any moment the Bolsheviks could be at the door, and all plans of escape would be forever a dream.

Anna hurriedly dresses in the clothes the gardener has secured for her to wear, clothes so they will look like a farm family going home from a trip to town. In the wagons, Joseph has packed as much warm clothing as he could in the small space. Joseph looks at Regina and tells her to get Anna and the kids to the shed where the loaded carriage is hidden. She nods her head in confirmation; she knows what needs to be done to leave. As he goes back through the house, he asks Chang if he will come along on the trip; they need his help with the babies. As a single man, he quickly agrees since he has always wanted to see China again.

When Joseph leaves the room, a terrified Anna starts to sob and shake. Regina firmly grasps her dear friend and sister-in-law by the shoulders and looks her straight in the eyes. She tells her she understands her terror, but they can no longer think of themselves. They both have to do what is best for the people they love. Regina tells Anna she will have to grow up from this moment and think of those three babies depending on her. There is only time for action, nothing else. Otherwise, she might be a woman with babies and no man for protection. Even naïve, sheltered Anna fully understands Regina's advice.

Joseph slips from the house through his beloved mother's rose garden. Later he will realize he did not even look at the garden when he went through it for the last time. Waiting for him is Wilbert the head gardener, Ernest the cook, and William one of the employees from the stables at the brewery. William is exceptionally good with horses and wagon repair. These three men are going along with the family. They had already heard about the arrests and knew the time to leave had arrived.

Joseph told them they would leave with the delivery wagons. Since William always works with the teams at the brewery, no one will become suspicious when he takes the horses from the stables. He makes several trips to the stable to get the horses for the wagons and the carriage. The stable foreman is a trusted friend, and Joseph has already discussed with him which horses will be used with what wagon and on the carriage. This is going to be a long and hard trip. They need the best horses the brewery has in the stables. Besides the money he has stashed in the hidden compartments he has built into the beer wagons, the horses and the wagons are the only thing of value he is taking from the brewery.

When William brings the first team, Joseph and the other men hitch them to one wagon while he goes to get the next set of horses. By the time he returns with the second team, the first wagon is ready to leave. William and the cook, dressed in brewery work clothes, get on the first wagon and drive it into the delivery line with the other beer wagons already in line to leave. As this is his usual job, it does not attract any unusual attention. He secures the wagon and goes back to the stable to get the last team of horses for the carriage. When he brings them to the shed, the second wagon is also ready to leave. The men shake hands and quickly ran through the plans where they will meet down the road from Saratov. They help Joseph hitch the team to the carriage. William and the gardener drive the second wagon into line, three wagons behind their other wagon. He gives the gardener the reins and returns to their first wagon.

Joseph prepares the carriage to leave. As he finishes with the last strap and secures the reins, he hears Anna, Regina, and Chang bringing the children from the house. Hettie just celebrated her second birthday a month ago and is excited about a ride in the countryside. Hettie is a very cooperative child. When she is told they all need to be quiet so they will not scare the horses, she tries her best to be quiet. She thinks it is fun to whisper instead of talking out loud.

Joseph can hear the delivery wagons get in line. It is a familiar sound this time of the morning at the brewery. He knows the ritual so well that he can tell who is doing what, where they are, and how they look. He knows they have only about 10 minutes before the train of wagons will move out. He wants to be ready to leave about the time half of the wagons have left when the dust the wagons stir up is in the air and there is a lot of commotion. He prays like he has never prayed in all his life that no one will notice they are leaving. He knows in his heart that Anna and Regina have also made contact with the Lord. They need His help.

He looks at his carriage and their clothes and is surprised at how different they look in their tattered old clothes. They do not look like the owner of the brewery and his usually fine family. He is pleased they look like they could be farmers even if they are in a carriage. He knows if he had tried this with Anna and the tiny babies in just a wagon, they would be doomed before they left. He has to hope and to pray the poor looking condition of the carriage will be enough to deter detection. After a quick goodbye to Regina, he takes the reigns. He knows the first several wagons have already left, and they need to move at any moment. Anna and Regina embrace and look into each other's eyes. There is so much to say with no time to say anything. They know if they start to sob like they want, Hettie will pick up on their desperation and get upset. They tell each other how much they love each other and they will see each other in a few days.

Chang is already in the carriage with the babies and Hettie. Regina helps Anna into the carriage and steps back to let them leave as tears roll down her cheeks and terror strikes her heart. She knows in her heart she should be in that carriage. Georg would have wanted her to leave. Her resolve was strong; she has to try to help him. Now that she is alone, she is so scared and unsure her plan will work. She also knows Anna desperately needs her in that carriage to help with those tiny, tiny little boys and Hettie. Precious Hettie! Regina knows she will miss her most of all, for they are kindred spirits. They have spent so many happy times together.

As Joseph pulls the wagon around the house into full view, his heart is in his throat, but he drives the team at a moderate rate like he would any other time they left the brewery. He really wants to make them run at top speed and get as far away as quickly as he can, but he knows better. He is relieved to see the stable foreman has created a diversion at the other end of the drive way. Everyone is looking in that direction and does not even notice when the brewery owner and his family leave for the last time. In reality, they all know that when the brewmaster leaves, the brewery is doomed, but he has been good to them. They know he has to leave, or he and his family will be killed.

So far so good, the farther they get from the brewery, the better Joseph feels. As they reach the edge of town, he sees no one behind them, and he relaxes a little. About a mile out of town, the wagons come into view way behind them. The plan is to travel separate from the wagons for the first days, so they will not attract attention. The two beer wagons driving together will not attract attention, but if the carriage is added to the group, people might take notice. They want to reduce the chance people might remember them if the Bolsheviks come and ask questions in the next few days. Joseph knows as slowly as they will travel with the carriage, if the Reds suspect which way they went, men on horseback could easily overtake them days or even weeks down the road. He is fairly certain they will look for them on the trains and roads to Eastern Europe or back to Moscow, where the family lived before they moved to the Volga River Valley, not in this direction.

Chapter 3

Joseph and Anna are on a road leading to a strange new land, Harbin, China, a place they have only heard about from travelers and read about in books. They know it is the international destination for refugees fleeing Russia. With every mile, their terror of being apprehended grows a little less intense. Joseph and Anna are leaving behind everything they know and love except for their three children. They are leaving behind their beloved Saratov and the family brewery. If it weren't for the constant threat of being captured, this would be an enjoyable trip. The countryside here in the Volga River Valley is full of the beautiful productive farms of the hard working German settlers. It is like driving through a picture.

Joseph is so glad Chang agreed to come along on the trip after Regina decided to stay in Saratov to try to get Georg out of prison. Joseph knows Anna has never taken care of herself, much less three little children. He is amazed she has fared so well this far. The children have cried only a few times, but together Chang and Anna took care of their problems, which is not a small feat if one considers the present circumstances. Apparently, Anna has taken Regina's warning to heart and is making a great effort.

A pallet has been brought along for the floor of the carriage. It is a comfortable place for Hettie to sleep and to play. There are two baskets with fluffy lamb's wool in the bottom for the twins. When the twins were born, Chang told Anna and Regina how Chinese mamas train their children to do their business in a bucket instead of in diapers. Regina loved the idea. With Regina's patience and natural ability to work with children along with Chang's instruction, the twins trained easily. Now the baskets stay dry, at least most of the time. Joseph also brought along a tall bottomless bucket for Anna to use to do her business along the road. He knew just squatting behind a bush would be too demoralizing for Anna. Anna is glad her milk for the babies has come in so generously. She has more than enough for the two little fellers. In fact, at times, she wants to wake them to nurse to get some relief for her breasts.

When the twins sleep, Anna and Hettie talk about the farm animals along the way. There are lots of slow-moving oxen pulling wagons loaded with the harvest to sell and people on their way home with supplies to stock up for the harsh winter just ahead. In each little village, there are chickens, ducks, dogs, and cats. At the edge of each village is a group of milk cows grazing. One person, either a milkmaid or a cowman, watches the cows for the village. As they pass the cattle, Hettie hangs out the window and waves wildly. The cowman or milkmaid responds with a vigorous wave in return. Everyone enjoys the exchange.

William grew up in the countryside, just outside of Saratov. He and Joseph have often discussed the back roads they are now traveling. Their goal is to stay off the main roads while still heading in the right direction.

Later in the day, they reach a small village as the workers from the small factories are getting off work. The workers step aside to give way for wagons to pass. However, Joseph and the other two drivers know if they get behind one of the milkmaids or a cowman bringing the cows home, they will just have to wait. The cows will take their good old time walking down the middle of the road, and no one is allowed to go through or around the cows. This afternoon they are really fortunate; there are only five cows left in the milkmaid's group when they get behind the procession of cows. Within a mile or so, all the cows turn in at their home farmyard, and the road is again clear for travel. Traveling at a slow pace for a little while is a nice break. Hettie enjoys the "cow parade." No one tells the cows anything; they just know when to leave the herd, turn into the cow trail or path leading to their owners' barns, and walk inside the barn.

The plan is to spend the night at the farm of William's cousins, the Wolthers, at the far edge of the Volga River Valley. As they reach the end of their first day on the road, the day is starting to give way to the night. The beer wagons pass the carriage and take the lead, so William can lead them to the Wolther's farm. As the wagons pass the carriage in a small village, they all wave and exchange pleasantries like strangers. The carriage then follows as far back as possible without losing sight of the beer wagons.

William has only been to this area once with his grandparents when he was a young boy. All those many years ago, the three of them stayed with the Wolters family for almost a week. During the stay, William and his cousin Ludwig explored the entire area, so he thinks he can find the farm without difficulty. As night approaches, he becomes apprehensive about finding the place in the dark. He says a quick prayer, and almost like magic, he begins to recognize the area. Through the years, William's mother Frieda exchanged long informative letters with Ludwig's mother Meta up until her death a year ago. William feels confident the family still lives in the same house and will not be sympathetic with the Communist movement.

The family farm is at the remote edge of a little settlement. William does not want to startle the family or arouse the neighbor's curiosity with all three wagons coming in at one time. As he approaches the farm, he signals Joseph to stop the carriage. Joseph pretends to check the carriage for repairs.

William plans to stop at the farm and talk to Ludwig. William remembers there was a large barn in the farmyard where the carriage can be hidden if the family's wagon is pushed outside. The plan works well; Ludwig is overjoyed to help his cousin help the Kara family escape from the Communists. They push the family wagon out into the farmyard. William signals Joseph to drive the carriage through the farmyard and into the barn before he stops. They hide the two beer wagons behind the barn between the huge fig trees. Ludwig's older boys take care of the tired horses with a good rub down and generous helpings of hay and grain. The older girls and the younger children scurry into the house to tell their mother about all the people staying for the night.

William's mother Frieda and Ludwig's mother Meta only met twice in their lives. Because of the long loving letters they had exchanged through the years, they were as close as sisters. Ludwig regards William as a brother and is so glad to see him. Ludwig and his family are very impressed to have Joseph, the brewmaster, and his family in their home, but the group is being treated as royalty because of the family's regard for William and his mother.

The weary travelers discover Ludwig's wife Ella is a fine cook. They are amazed how she made such tasty food appear almost as if she had grabbed it out of thin air. Her family whole heartedly agrees with their observation of her skill as a cook. It is obvious they are proud of her gift to quickly make great food out of limited ingredients.

Ludwig loves to tell stories, especially funny ones. With the warm hospitality, funny stories, and plentiful food, it is an evening to remember. The long wooden table with benches on each side is crowded with the adults. The children are sent out on the porch to eat. When they hear the laughter, they come back inside to hear the stories. After the meal and the stories, Joseph and Ludwig discuss a business arrangement. Joseph explains how he had to leave without a lot of the last minute things he planned to bring like fresh fruits and vegetables. He had some dried meats and fruit already on the wagon but not nearly as much as he had planned. It is going to be a long trip to China with so many mouths to feed. Ludwig assures him he will give him all he can spare. Joseph understands the normal country generosity but feels he wants to pay the family, so he can take more to last the entire trip. Ludwig tells him about the Sims farm along the road they will be traveling. He feels they will also have extra supplies Joseph can buy the next day.

Joseph has the large chest of money in the hidden compartment on the beer wagon. Joseph is glad he had Regina sew Anna's jewels into the linings of their winter coats, which are packed in the trunk on the back of the carriage. He thinks about how he did that mostly to humor Anna since she loves her jewelry. Some are really exquisite pieces she brought along from Prague. Little does he know, as history will unfold, they will be the family's salvation. He and Ludwig reach an agreement on the supplies, and while Joseph goes to bed feeling much better about the trip, the idea of his brothers sitting in prison is always heavy on his mind.

As is the custom in the German homes in the area, when guests arrive, the children of the family are relegated to sleep on the floor or in the barn. Then the company, especially the female guests and little babies, can be in the house. As this family home is not large, the children will be out in the barn along with the drivers. William declines the offer to stay in the house. Chang will sleep on the floor to help take care of the babies when they awake in the night. Ludwig decides to sleep in the barn with the men, so he can spend as much time as possible with William. Also, with two small babies in the house, he thinks he will probably get a better night's sleep in the barn.

William and Ludwig talk and laugh into the night, sharing memories. Ludwig asks William if he is still so good with the slingshot. They talk about how they hunted rabbits when William came to visit with his grandparents. William tells Ludwig about the slingshot competition they had annually in Saratov. William had taken the trophy many times, but the Communists stopped the competition.

It is not long before everyone in the barn is sound asleep. It was a hard, trying day, full of imminent danger and possible death if discovered. They know there is danger, so Ludwig's older children take turns, two at a time, watching the road in the direction of Saratov. If riders approach the farm, the farm has a big root cellar big enough to hold a lot of people, but they will need time to get everyone across the farmyard before the riders would get to the farm.

The next morning, long before the sun even thinks about coming up, the entire farmyard is alive with activity. Joseph and his family plan on being on the road by the first gray light of dawn. The babies slept better than usual; evidently the ride wore them out as much as the grown ups.

Hettie keeps asking for Tanta Regina and Uncle Georg. Every time she mentions them, it breaks Joseph's heart. He blames himself for letting Alois talk him into waiting another day. If only he had insisted, his brothers would be with him now, not in some stinky prison cell in Saratov. It is tearing his heart out to think of their situation. Who will bring them food? How will they exist? He has a small glimmer of hope that Regina will be able to get them freed with her family's connections, but in the depths of his heart, he knows Igor Ivanson is a vicious man with no scruples. Joseph even worries about Regina's safety, but he pushes the thought to the back of his mind.

They leave the farm with a fond farewell and the Lord's blessings. The whole troop is refreshed and in good spirits. Even Anna enjoyed the Wolters family. Joseph is so proud of her for being so pleasant with Ella and her daughters, not even one condescending remark from her that he knows about. Ludwig's stories had been so humorous because he can see past the hard times and bad situations to the funny side of stories after they happen. The conversations around the table the night before had opened Anna's eyes to the possible dangers ahead of them. She has decided to enjoy the safety of the situation. She knows they can't go back. Her friends told her many stories of prominent families being brutally murdered after the women, sometimes almost infant girls, had been raped repeatedly. The men had been humiliated by being forced to watch. Then the family would be killed slowly, one at a time. Occasionally, one member would be allowed to live, so they could spread the stories and create terror in the people. They all knew they had to leave.

When they stop at the Sims farm for more supplies, Joseph is glad they can pay. The family looks like they can use the money more than the extra food they have accumulated. Joseph also bought extra lamb's wool skins for the babies. Everyone knows that soon the farms will get few and far between and the farmers might not have extra to sell.

As they get back on the road, to give Anna a break, Joseph lets Hettie come up and sit with him on the driver's seat. She is such an enjoyable child. Her wit and keen observation of everything is like a breath of fresh air for Joseph. As they talk, he knows it will not be long before she will figure out this is not just a little outing. The two talk about a lot of things they see along the road. Again, she asks about Regina and Georg. Joseph decides that when he gets to Harbin, he will find a mercenary to go back and get his brothers out of prison. He is again lost in the thought that they should have left a day sooner.

All of a sudden, he is brought back by the sound of Hettie calling to him from a distance. "Daddy, look at me!!! See what I can do!" He is horror struck! There is his little dancer standing on the tong of the carriage, the moving hinged piece of wood at the bottom edge of the carriage front connecting the horses to the carriage. He knows if the carriage hits a bump, as it is sure to do any minute, she will be thrown to the ground. Landing on the ground at this speed will surely be deadly. Even if she survives the fall, the team of horses on the wagon behind them will trample her before William, the driver, can react and stop his team of horses.

His first reaction is to reach for her, but he instinctively knows any sudden movement of the reins will confuse and excite the horses. He knows he has to take his time and get Hettie to come back up to the seat on her own power. He tells her, "Daddy is so proud of you!! Let's see if you can grab my feet and come back up to sit here with me." He braces himself to make sure his feet are firmly on the front edge of the carriage. He calmly instructs her, "Grab my foot so you are between my feet." She grabs his foot, then his pant leg, and pulls herself up between his feet. She scampers right up his legs and sits down on the seat next to him. She is sitting there just like she has been there all along, smiling at her accomplishment!

She exclaims, "Daddy, that was fun!"

Joseph signals William to stop. Without a word, he gives Hettie a big long hug. Then he asks her to jump down and join her mother in the carriage. She slips off the seat and gets into the carriage. She is talking a mile a minute to anyone or no one in particular. As soon as Hettie climbs into the carriage, tears begin to flow down Joseph's face. He is overtaken with emotions he has held in check for so long. He had just come so close to such a tragedy. How would he have faced Anna? How would he have lived without his precious Hettie? The stress of the last several days and the imprisonment of his brothers overwhelms this strong man like a flooding river raging out control. His body shakes with sobs as the tears stream down his face.

As soon as Hettie gets in the carriage, she exclaims, "Mama, you should have seen me. I was down dancing with the horses!" Anna does not have time to say anything before they hear Joseph crying. Hettie asks, "Why is Daddy crying? I thought he was so proud of me dancing with the horses!"

Anna answers as tears flow down her cheeks, "He is so happy you are still alive and we are having such a good trip."

The tears are good for Joseph; he feels like a great weight has been lifted from his shoulders. He has to face facts; they did not leave a day earlier. Now he can also see that he made a lot of good decisions. If they had not left when they did, he would now be dead or sitting next to his brothers in prison, and Anna and the children would be dead or slaves. He realizes he can no longer afford the luxury of looking back. The brewery his father built is history. They are on the road to a future totally unknown and scary, but they are alive and well. He needs to keep that fact as his driving force.

As he gets control of his emotions, he tells William, "From now on we need to leave more distance between the wagon and the carriage." He shares with William what almost happened. William looks pale and horror-struck at how terrible it would have been to see and be part of what could have happened.

Chapter 4

As they knew it would, when they get farther into Siberia, the settlements give way to wilderness. The roads are rough and dangerous. Joseph is so impressed with Anna, for she is easier to work with then he can ever remember. She is like the frontier women, the ancestors talked about when the Germans came over centuries ago to the Volga River Valley. She is nursing the babies, and while she is producing less milk, it is still more then enough for the little boys, who are thriving. She and Chung have developed a schedule for the boys to nurse and to sleep that is working so well.

All along the trail and especially at night, a few wolves are always lurking in the distance. When the group stops at farms along the way to spend the night, they hear stories of huge packs of wolves attacking wagons even in the broad daylight. So far, all they have seen are a few wolves together. When they have to spend the night on the road, the men keep a large fire going all night to keep the wolves at a distance. They have a rifle along, but the bullets are scarce, only to be used as a last resort since they will not be able to buy bullets along the road. They need the bullets to shoot animals to eat. William uses his sling shot on any wolf getting too close to the wagons or their campfire at night. The more he practices, the better his aim becomes. Now he can bring down a wolf at close range. Around the campfire, it is part of the night noises to hear the wolves feasting on or fighting over the wolf carcass. With the meat from the dead wolf to eat, the wolves are not as aggressive around the campfire. They all know if a really big pack attacks the three wagons, it will be a real fight for survival. So far, so good!

Last night it snowed almost all night, so this morning there is a blanket of white snow as far as the eye can see. They cannot see the road! After they study the situation, they realize the road is the only area completely without vegetation since it is winding through an area of trees and scrub brush. For the first few hours, the caravan travels slower than usual, making sure they are really on the road. About midmorning they meet a local farmer's son coming in the opposite direction. He is traveling faster in the deep snow because he knows where the road makes turns. Now the way will be easier.

Joseph asks the young man, "Do you know if there might be someone from this area I can hire as a guide to ride along with our group through the snow?"

He replies, "You can follow my tracks back to my village now. When you get there, ask for Yon Schmidt. He will probably be able to guide you for a couple of days, at least until you can find another guide down the road." He adds, "Yon is a hunter and trapper and knows the whole area like the back of his hand, and he will be grateful for the chance to make a little money."

The trip through the snow to the village is much faster and easier. Joseph decides if Yon cannot help them, he will look until he finds someone else. It is just too dangerous driving these big wagons and the carriage without knowing the road.

When they find Yon, his horse is already saddled, and his supplies are packed because he is ready to leave on a hunting trip. He is willing to change his plans to help the Karas. Yon ties his horse behind the carriage and climbs on the carriage seat with Joseph. The road ahead is easy to see now that people have come into town and marked the trail, but there are still misleading side roads leading to farms. Joseph is already glad they have Yon along to keep them in the right direction. Yon tells Joseph about his village, larger than most, with several businesses and a Lutheran church. They have a school and a good doctor. Yon loves to talk and to tell stories.

As they travel down the road, the deep snow on the road is marked by several wagons. Yon tells Joseph he knows who is in some of the wagons ahead because they left his village early this morning. The story he relates is about a group of wagons from a village a hard day's ride ahead. Early this morning while Yon was getting supplies, two of the couples from one of the wagons came into the dry goods store. They had come into town to get supplies for their little settlement and to buy material for wedding dresses. The two couples are getting married in a few weeks in a double ceremony. The young men, Chas and Henry, are about Yon's age, and the girls, identical twins Kerry Ann and Mary Ann, are a little younger. Yon thinks it is a good thing Kerry Ann, the sister betrothed to Chas, wears her braids of slightly darker hair on the top of her head while Mary Ann wears her slightly lighter hair in one braid falling down her back so he can easily tell them apart. Yon really likes Chas because he is a nice fella with a serious but friendly attitude.

Yon tells Joseph how much he enjoyed the young women's excitement as they picked out the material for their wedding dresses; the twins talk a mile a minute as they laugh and plan their special day. While the ladies shop, Chas tells Yon about his concern for Henry, the young man betrothed to Mary Ann. This morning the young man is not interested in wedding plans. He can not stand still; he is wringing his hands and mumbling to himself with a wild look in his eyes. Chas tells Yon that Henry had been attacked by wolves two years ago and almost died. On the trip into town yesterday, they saw a few wolves, and now he is terrified to travel home. Yon feels so sorry for the young man. He can tell from Chas' comments that the young man is usually rational, but today he is so upset that he appears to be losing hold of his sanity. Chas is trying to keep him calm, so the twins can enjoy shopping. Chas tells Henry repeatedly he just needs to get a hold of himself. He reminds Henry that shopping for the wedding dress material is a once in a lifetime event for the sisters and he wants them to enjoy this special time together in town.

Yon talks to Mary Ann as he helps them load their wagon with their supplies. Unable to focus long enough to help with the loading, Henry paces back and forth on the store porch, and his mumbling is beginning to sound more like gibberish. Chas tells him to be quiet before he scares everyone. On their wagon they have a big old heavy trunk with a domed lid. Chas tells Yon the trunk came along from Germany with the girls' grandparents when they came to Russia. Sarcastically, he says he did not want to bring that big old thing along, but the twins' mother insisted they bring it along to keep the wedding dress material out of the weather. As they load, the ladies carefully put their treasured bolts of cloth, lace, thread, and other special supplies in the trunk. Yon notices their wagon is bigger than most wagons used by the local farmers, but their horses are big and strong enough to pull the load. Yon helps Chas bring out the sacks of their sand they warmed under the wood stove in the store. As they leave town following the two other wagons from their little village, the girls are sitting cozily on the warmed sandbags wrapped in their thick quilts. Wrapped in a thick, warm quilt, Chas is on the driver's seat while next to him, a scared Henry sits on his quilt.

As he relates the story to Joseph, Yon remarks several times how much he likes the twin Mary Ann, and he tells Joseph more than once every word the young lady spoke to him back at the store. He tells him about her smile, her sweet voice, and her beauty. He confides in Joseph that he cannot get her out of his mind. Women usually never interest him, but for some reason he does not understand, this young lady is always in his thoughts. Yon says he sure wishes she was not betrothed. He asks Joseph if a woman has ever had that effect on him. Joseph smiles remembering when he met Anna and how he knew from the first moment he saw her she was the one he wanted to marry. Joseph feels sad Yon is too late to claim his chosen lady.

The Kara wagons follow the wagon's tracks for most of the day. Then Yon notices the tracks indicate the wagons ahead started running, and he can see why. There are wolf tracks indicating a huge pack alongside the wagon and horse tracks. Yon remarks about the size of Chas' wagon, and he fears they won't be as fast as the other wagons. Soon they notice supplies lying all over the road: bags of sugar, flour, cans of tobacco, and sand bags, and they know the families threw the supplies out to lighten the load so that the wagon could go faster. They stop and pick up what is still usable, but when they find the bolts of wedding dress material, they know Chas' wagon is the one under attack. Joseph feels so sorry for Yon; he can see his heart is breaking.

As they piece together the story of what is happening to the wagon up ahead, Joseph shouts to Anna for Hettie to crawl into the hiding spot under the seat. He instructs Anna to cover the windows and not to look out for any reason. Yon wants to run the horses at top speed, but Joseph keeps the horses at a reasonably fast pace. They started out hours behind the wagons under attack, so he feels whatever their fate, they can never reach them in time to help. Joseph dreads what they will find farther up the road, and he wishes now he had not brought Yon along, knowing how he feels about the young lady in the wagon that is probably doomed.

Farther down the road, they are met with a horrible sight. The white snow is streaked with blood, and there are bones scattered in every direction. There is so little left that it is hard to tell what has been killed, but there is one lone old wolf chewing inside the top of a man's work boot. Yon recognizes the hat snagged on a scrub bush as belonging to Henry, the young man he met at the dry goods store, Mary's intended. As they draw near the horrible scene, the scraggly old wolf does not run. He is either too old to run or too hungry to leave any morsel still in the shoe. Joseph cannot resist and shoots the beast between those evil green eyes with one of his treasured bullets. At the sound of the gunshot, Anna lifts the curtain and sees the horrible scene. She screams, and they can hear her vomit. They stop, and Joseph and Chang help Anna clean up the mess inside the carriage. Yon and the other drivers look closer at the horrible bloody mess along the road in the snow. They discover why it had been so hard to determine what had been killed when they first approached the scene. The men realize a huge wolf had also been eaten along with the man. Joseph and Anna discuss not continuing, but they have no choice. Anna tells Joseph next time she will heed his warning when he tells her not to look out the window. As they continue down the road, she holds her babies and talks to Hettie. Now, she knows firsthand how much danger lies out here in the wilderness.

The Kara wagons don't go far when they come over a rise in the road. They can see ahead for miles. There at the bottom of the hill is a horrible scene. Chas' wagon only made it to the bottom of the hill. The horses are just a pile of bones in the center of a huge scarlet stain on the snow in every direction. They can see there is a lot of blood spattered inside the wagon and on the old trunk standing on end with the lid open. Yon starts to cry as there is no sign of human life and no sign of the other wagons that had been ahead of Chas' wagon. Most of the wolves are getting full and leaving, and only a few wolves remain. As they approach, the last wolf leaves the area. When they get closer to the gruesome scene, they cannot believe what they are seeing; it is something close to a miracle. The old trunk on the wagon starts to move, and now that they are closer, they can see the trunk is standing on end with the lid opened up against the back of the wagon seat. As they watch, Chas and Kerry Ann crawl out from under the seat. As they both push the trunk away from the seat, Mary Ann crawls out of the trunk. Yon, Joseph, and all the men cheer. Joseph shouts to Anna, "The people are alive!" Yon jumps off the carriage and runs down the hill to Mary Ann, sweeping her up in his strong arms and swinging her around as he shouts, cries, and laughs. Joseph chuckles to himself under his breath at what he figures is a very uncharacteristic spontaneous show of affection for Yon since he did not know she existed when he got up this morning. Mary Ann is so glad to be safe that she does not appear to question Yon's exuberant celebration.

As they reach the wagon, everyone is shouting or crying with joy. No one expected to find anyone alive, much less three of them almost without a scratch even though they are covered in dried blood. Together they tell the story of their ordeal. When the wolves first start chasing us, we are all so scared, but poor Henry is so terrified he is useless. To lighten the load Chas wants to get rid of the trunk, but he is afraid at the speed they are traveling the girls will not be able to get the heavy trunk over the high sides of the wagon without falling out themselves. So, Chas tells them to throw out all the supplies, including everything in the trunk, but to keep the trunk and their quilts, so they can wrap up in them for some protection. Chas says that as the wolves get closer, Henry starts to get a little control of himself. As the horses begin losing ground to the snarling growling slobbering creatures with such tremendous speed, one of the biggest wolves jumps into the back of the wagon, bearing his teeth as he heads for the twins under the wagon seat. Without so much as a second's hesitation, Henry grabs his big knife out of the holder sewn on his pants leg and jumps into the back of the wagon between the wolf and the girls. As the wolf lunges forward, Henry slashes with his knife and catches the wolf across the mouth. Although it is momentarily stunned, the animal is so strong and has so much momentum that in an instant his huge paws are on Henry's shoulders. As they scuffle, Henry thrusts his big knife into the wolf's underside as blood and guts explode out of the animal all over the wagon. As the huge beast loses strength, his enormous weight pushes Henry to the edge of the wagon, and they are thrown off the wagon. For the rest of their lives, everyone in the wagon will remember the blood curdling scream as he and the wolf hit the rocky ground along the road. All three agree that at the point of impact with the ground, his scream stops as he either dies or is unconscious on impact before he is enveloped in the swarm of ravenous wolves.

The wolves chasing the horses gain speed and determination with the smell of the fresh blood and the excitement of the kill. Chas says at this point he knows they are not going to be able to out-run the wolves. He tells the girls to pull the trunk as close as they can behind the wagon seat. As their horses are overtaken by the wolves and start to go down, Chas jumps into the back of the wagon. He opens the trunk, stands it on end, and tells Mary Ann to get in the trunk as he joins Kerry Ann under the wagon seat. With the trunk lid still open, he and Kerry Ann manage to pull it up against the seat with super-human strength to form a small but safe hiding spot. They sit in their cramped positions for hours trying not to make a sound. They know the trunk is just pulled up to the back of the seat, and if the strong wolves start scratching and pushing on the trunk, it will be impossible for the three inside to keep it up against the wagon seat because there is no place inside the trunk to get a secure hold. They watch through the cracks as the wolves attack and fight each other as they devour the horses. After what seams like an eternity, the last wolf leaves the area about the same time as they hear the Kara wagons approach.

After hearing the details of the story several times and things calm down a little, Joseph is so pleased to say he and Yon had been able to save some of the supplies they had thrown out, but he keeps the material hidden because now the beautiful material will just be a point of pain for Mary Ann. They find out that Mary Ann and Henry had been sweethearts from childhood. She cannot envision her life without him, but she is so proud of his bravery. Despite his tremendous fear of the wolves, he had come to her rescue without a moment's thought to his own safety, and it cost him his life. Like a big family, they all travel to their village for a celebration of the lives saved and a tribute to the heroic life lost. Little did they know, the event will take a tragic toll on the Kara caravan and will permeate throughout the family's history.

There is a young trapper Waldemar in the village. He knows about a man Alois Becker, who was reported to be smuggling wagons across the Amur River into China a few days earlier. Joseph hires Waldemar to lead them through the snow to the smuggler. When they get near the Chinese border, he plans on dividing the remaining supplies. Then he plans on sending all the drivers back with Waldemar to return to Saratov. Joseph smiles a knowing smile when Yon offers to stay in the village so he can help the drivers on their way back to Saratov. Chung, who is a Chinese citizen, will drive one wagon and help them with the language when they get into the city of Harbin.

Chapter 5

As they start out bright and early the next morning, they are all in high spirits. Anna notices she has less milk for the morning feeding. Chung tells her the shock of the encounter with the wolves the day before might have affected her production of milk, but he feels it will correct itself in short order. However, as the day progresses, she produces less and less milk to feed the twins. Because of the basic hardships of the harsh Siberian landscape, the trip has been difficult for everyone the last few weeks, but now with at least one baby always crying and everyone knowing a horrible situation is developing, the trip becomes a real nightmare without end.

With Waldemar's guidance, it is easier than they expected to find Alois, the smuggler. Alois was born and raised near the river and personally knows some of the guards. He knows when they take their lunch break and the section of the river just out of their line of view while they eat lunch.

Joseph and the drivers divide the supplies. One wagon will go with the carriage, and the other will go back home. William insists they leave his portion of the supplies on the main wagon because he will not go back. He stays with the Karas to drive the extra wagon. With the babies crying almost non-stop, he knows Chung needs to be in the carriage, or the guards will be alerted with the crying babies. He also knows it is still a long trip to Harbin; the crisis with the babies is just going to get worse.

Anna waits until just the last minute to feed the babies the milk she has, so they will be quiet as they cross the river. What she has is enough for both babies to be content for a little while. Anna holds one, and Chung holds the other as they cross. The river is frozen, and with only two wagons, they are quickly across the river in the middle of the day. Their monumental accomplishment of crossing the river into China is over shadowed by the crisis with the babies, which is getting worse with each passing hour.

Joseph and Anna finally have to make a horrible decision. They love both of the beautiful little boys, but they both can see she is going to have to feed one twin more, or neither one will be alive when they reach Harbin.

When she was growing up in Prague, Anna's parents always had favorites. Showing partiality was just a fact of life; it was how things were done through the generations in her family. She was her father's favorite, and her younger sister was her mother's favorite. She has a favorite twin, Hans, the second born, so it is not a question as to which twin will get more. Actually, she began somewhat favoring Hans over Max as soon as the milk started getting short.

Joseph grew up in a family where there were no favorites. For him, it is a horrible decision, but Anna has already made the decision for him. It is a horrible next several days. They are all like walking dead, knowing full well that no matter what they do, one of the little boys is probably going to die.

When they finally reach Harbin, Max is a very weak and sick little boy, but he is alive. They find doctors in Harbin, who try everything they know to save the little boy, but he dies the next day. Joseph and Anna are devastated. Joseph had been so proud to have twin boys. Now he feels if he had done something else, anything else, maybe then his little boy would still be alive.

They are in a refugee city with people from all over Russia. All of them are in the same situation as Joseph and Anna, except Joseph has the stash of money. Most of the other refugees have nothing but the coats on their backs. Joseph is able to pay for a little place for them to stay, not an expensive hotel but a clean place out of the cold. He knows he has to start looking for a place with spring-fed water to build a new brewery. His first order of business, before he starts work on the brewery, is to hire a mercenary to return to Russia to get Georg and Alois out of prison and to find Regina. He is so thankful he has money.

As Joseph travels around Harbin, it becomes apparent that there is very little beer brewed in China. In his opinion, the ones he tastes are not as good as the beer he and his brothers brew. He becomes friends with an affluent Chinese businessman named Tam. Much to Joseph's surprise, Tam knows about his beer. Some of Tam's friends had traveled to Russia, and when they returned, they raved about Joseph's Five Star beer. Joseph and Tam talk at length about his brew and how it will take time for the people in China to get used to the different taste of Joseph's beer. Joseph knows a lot of the refugees here in Harbin are of German decent, and they will take to his beer like a long lost friend. Joseph also knows that unless he can get Chinese men to like his beer, he will have difficulty making a huge success of his brewery.

As Joseph and Tam become friends, they come upon the solution to the problem. Tam will become a partner in the brewery. Joseph will brew the beer, and Tam will market it among his friends and business associates. Tam knows of a piece of land for sale in Peking with an abundant flow of spring water that is owned by a friend of his Mr. Cho. Joseph and Tam discuss the location. Peking has a large permanent population of Europeans. The European population here in Harbin will probably leave eventually, taking with them a good chunk of the beer lovers. Joseph likes the idea that Anna could have European people to socialize with in Peking. Tam sends a message to his friend in Peking to come to Harbin to make the deal.

Joseph is a little leery as to why Mr. Cho is coming to Harbin, instead of them going to Peking and looking at the land. Tam skirts the question and never really gives an answer that satisfies Joseph. About this time, all Russian paper money is declared worthless! Instead of being a wealthy man purchasing a piece of land, Joseph is a man with a chest of worthless paper money. Tam has gotten so excited about the idea of making the great tasting German Beer in China that he works with Joseph despite his money problems. Instead of cash, Joseph has Anna's jewelry. Originally, Joseph had no plans to use her jewelry, but now he knows he has no choice.

Tam takes the jewelry as Joseph's contribution toward the purchase price of the land and the construction of the brewery in Peking. He will also front Joseph the money to live on while the brewery is being built. Tam will keep the jewelry, and Joseph can buy it back when the brewery becomes successful.

Joseph is glad he had not sold the carriage or the horses. They are better horses than anything he sees in China. With all his worthless money, the carriage is all he can afford for transportation now. Joseph, Anna, Hettie, Hans, and Chang pack up their meager belongings. William has taken the beer wagon back to Saratov. The Karas in their tattered carriage and Tam in his fine carriage leave for Peking.

Chapter 6

They stay in country inns along the road; Tam pays all the bills, which is hard for Joseph. He can feel himself becoming obligated to Tam and losing control of the business end of this arrangement, but Tam always treats him with the utmost respect. All the people he talked to around Harbin referred to Tam as an honest man. At this point, Joseph feels he has to trust someone.

When they get to the walled city of Peking, it is like a different world. They stay in the center of the city in the beautiful home of Tam's friend, Mr. Cho, the landowner. Anna is overjoyed as they are treated like royalty. They are encouraged to rest for a day from the long travel before they go to the property. Joseph is anxious to see the property, but he realizes he is really going to have very little choice except to buy the property. Everything they are telling him about the property sounds perfect. The spring water is pristine and plentiful. They will be just a little way outside the wall, and there is a railroad almost at the edge of the property. When they make more than they can sell in Peking, the railroad can build a spur into or right in front of the property to transport their beer all over China.

Anna enjoys living like a wealthy lady again; she even has a nurse to look after Hans and Hettie while she relaxes and strolls through the beautiful garden. Joseph takes the day to enjoy the smile on Anna's face. He especially enjoys their strolls through the garden. Even though many of the plants are different from the plants in his mother's garden, it is like connecting with a part of his life that is now so distant. At dusk, he returns to the garden alone and finds the peace and tranquility he so desperately needs. His load of decisions in the negotiations for the land and the construction of the new brewery are heavy on his shoulders. He trusts Tam, but he still feels there is something he does not know. He can feel the undertow of something, and it is making him very uncomfortable.

That evening, the party held in their honor is a grand affair with the house full of important people. It does not take long for Joseph and Anna to realize they are socializing with the elite of Peking. Many of the people are from the Legation, the European section of the city. Earlier in the day, they toured that part of the city; it was just like being in Europe. Every language can be heard at the party. Anna and Joseph feel they are really going to enjoy living here in Peking, especially when they have money again and Anna can give parties and entertain the cream of society.

The next morning, they all travel outside the wall to the property. As they approach the land, Joseph's heart sinks into his stomach. He and Anna look at each other in total disbelief. The land is surrounded by a large fence with jagged broken glass on the top to keep people out. As they drive through the large ornate iron gates opened by a guard, they cannot believe their eyes. The land is an old cemetery for the wealthy.

When they express their shock, Tam and Mr. Cho express no concern over the graves. They can be dug up; the plots with people still around will have the bodies moved to another cemetery. They assure Joseph they will arrange for the graves to be removed. They will hire coolies to dig up the graves and to remove all the bodies and tombstones.

Joseph and Ann come from a society where cemeteries are sacred and never to be disturbed, but Joseph knows he has no choice. He cannot back out because Tam has Anna's jewelry in Harbin and his money is worthless. Other than the graves, the land is exactly what he needs to build the brewery. With a reluctant heart, he agrees to proceed with Tam and the partnership. When they approach Mr. Cho, he offers to become a third partner, using the land as his part of the investment. They reach an agreement on the percentage each will have in the business.

There is a small care-taker's home on the property, just a little more than a shack in Anna's eyes. Joseph decides they will live in the house while the brewery is being built. Anna is not happy about the idea, but she knows they have no money, leaving her no choice. It will be better than living in the carriage on the road. At least they will have a roof over their heads. Tam agrees to stay in Peking for several months to work with Joseph to remove the graves and to order the supplies and equipment for the new brewery.

Joseph and Anna quickly learn the rules of going in and out of the city wall. From conversations and observations, they soon know going outside the main city wall can be dangerous. The rules are strongly enforced because the gangs and thieves rule outside the wall, especially after dark. At dusk, the gates are closed to everyone except a few prominent people with passes issued by the government. Otherwise, no one is allowed in or out until daylight the next day. If you get caught on the wrong side, you just have to make other arrangements until the morning, no exceptions for the average person. Tam begins the process to get a pass for Joseph, and it appears the officials like the idea of a good German brewery being built here in China.

Tam tells Joseph he has hired a large group of coolies, the lowest paid unskilled workers in Chinese society, to dig up the graves. He expressly tells Joseph to stay out of the way of the grave movers. He explains the graves contain wealthy people and their concubines, who were buried with their valuables.

This explains the big fence and armed guard always on duty at the cemetery.

As the graves are dug up, the coolies fight each other over the valuables they unearth. They kill each other like flies. No authorities come, and no one thinks it is a problem. The workers take the newly dead coolies and the old unclaimed bodies from the graves and throw them to the "Holy Dogs" in a trench at the edge of town. Whoever ends up with the valuables is the winner. This goes on until the graves are all removed.

The process makes Joseph sick to his stomach. He cannot believe he will be living and raising his young family among people with such little regard for human life. There are two totally different worlds here in China: the world inside the wall and the world outside the wall. To keep their families and belongings safe, successful people living outside the main wall build tall walls with broken grass on the top around their properties and keep a constant vigil.

Chang and some coolies clean the little house and make it ready for the family. The family that lived there for years is moving. Joseph is there when they came back for the last of their belongings. They repeatedly caution Joseph he will have to keep his rifle handy at all times. The man warns, "Living here in this place is worse than living out in Siberia." Joseph and Chang look at each other and shiver in their boots. The man does not know how much they understand the analogy. He tells them the Chinese people living in the area resent outsiders moving into the area He shows them places to watch and how to recognize the sound of digging under the fence at night. He tells Joseph he will have to hire a guard and be willing to shoot to kill a few times, or they will be over run by the thugs in the area. He also tells them the officials will not come. They have to take care of the thieves themselves. Joseph is thankful Tam hired the old guards from the cemetery as soon as the graves were cleared and the new construction materials started arriving. Without the guards, the little hovel they are living in would not be safe for Anna and the children.

Chapter 7

The Five Star Brewery also called the Son Ho Shin Brewery is completed between 1910 and 1911. The first batch is a trial run, and only a select few are invited to taste. Tam has invested a huge fortune into the brewery and returns from Harbin to taste the results. No one is disappointed; it is superb. Tam and Mr. Cho throw a big party for all their friends. It is obvious the new Five Star Beer is going to be a success, especially for the Europeans inside the Legation. Tam's Chinese friends are also impressed with the beer. The three partners agree to add the other vats and storage areas for the brewery to increase capacity. Everyone can see it is going to be a lucrative venture.

Lavish entertaining is the main concern in the design of the new house here outside the wall of Peking. They have to have accommodations available for their guests, or Anna's parties have to be early in the day. As the sun begins to set, the guests returning to Peking will have to leave before the gate closes for the day or spend the night. Joseph has a pass to go in and out the gate, but it is for Joseph and no one else.

The house is going to be large and ornate. From the drive way, dual stairs lead up to the first landing then up to a large veranda on the second level. The main grand entrance foyer will open up to a thirty-foot ceiling with stairs on each side, leading up to the bedrooms on the third floor. A railed balcony circles the foyer and meets again at the rear wide steps leading back down into the foyer. There will be a statue of Christ at the top of the stairs. Each of the four upstairs bedrooms will have direct access to the balcony. The main level includes a large ballroom and a huge dining room for entertaining, and three large bedrooms down stairs. The house is surrounded by a large formal garden with roses and other beautiful flowers. A compound for the little animals for the children is at the back of the property.

The Karas join the Peking Country Club in the Legation, and Anna is again in her element. With the new brewery making quite a stir in the community, Joseph and Anna are on the top of the most coveted invitation lists. Their new friends in the Legation have no idea Anna and Joseph are living in less than elegant surroundings. Unless she is socializing with her new friends in the Legation, Anna spends much of her time at the brewery, so she can keep a close eye on the construction of the new house. Joseph is still working on getting the brewery complete. They use the worthless paper money from Russia to paper the walls in Joseph's study. For the next thirty years, he enjoys showing everyone the walls with the worthless money. Things are looking up for the Kara family.

Joseph develops a camel train (wagons pulled by camels) to deliver his beer in areas not serviced by the train. At capacity, the brewery will have 200 employees on rotating shifts. The workers, who live on the grounds during their shifts, meet each morning in front of the second floor veranda of the house for the orders for the day from Brewmaster Kara.

Chang takes care of the children, Hans and Hettie. Hans, the twin that remains, is a beautiful blue-eyed little boy with curly blond hair and an exceptionally pleasant disposition. Anna enrolls Hettie in dance and piano lessons in the Legation. Her teachers can see she has special musical talent. She has the God-given ability to perform for a large group or just one person. People fall in love with the talented little girl who plays and dances with such enthusiasm and grace.

The family joins St. Joseph Catholic Church in Peking and attends church every Sunday, rain or shine, before heading to the club for lunch. Even though the twins had been baptized in Harbin before Max died, the Karas redo the baptism, so they can have a party like they had for Hettie's baptism in Saratov. Anna enjoys giving the celebratory meal for their church friends at the country club after the service. Entertaining is her passion, and she begins to feel alive again.

Anna is speaking less and less about the dead twin. Joseph is so glad her sanity has survived the loss. There were times in the last few months he had been concerned by the wild, distant look in her eyes. Now his heart is getting lighter; she appears to be fine. Sometimes, however, he just does not understand why she always needs to be so busy. She never allows herself time to relax or just sit and talk with him like they did on the trip through Siberia. He misses her company, but with all the change and grief in their lives, he is glad she appears happy again.

To celebrate the completion of their new home, they give a party for all their friends and business associates. It is a wonderful occasion with big band music, dancing, wonderful food, and fine wines. Anna makes no bones about the fact that beer is not an appropriate refreshment at her parties.

While living in the little hut, they experienced the dust storms from the Gobi desert that lasted for days at a time. When the family got up in the morning, their heads were outlined on the pillow by dust. They learned unless tightly sealed in a jar or a well-sealed trunk, everything becomes covered in a layer of red dust. So, in the new house Anna's closet is lined with ornate hand engraved wooden chests, things of beauty, but they are there to protect her clothes.

Having guests is becoming a way of life at the Kara home. Many times the guests stay for days. Anna is the perfect hostess, always busy making sure the household staff takes care of everyone's needs. Joseph enjoys the company, but he is becoming weary of the constant parade of friends. Sometimes he feels guilty they have so many visitors and friends while his brothers are sitting in prison. The mercenary was unsuccessful in his attempt to rescue the brothers. To keep his mind occupied, Joseph spends his time at the brewery or in his study doing paper work. Despite his guilty feelings, life is good.

Chapter 8

The household mail is delivered in the foyer of their home. Sometimes Joseph is the first to see the mail, sometimes Anna. One Wednesday afternoon, they are coming home from a luncheon at the club when they see a letter from Joseph's cousin Lela in Prague. Anna is so glad to see the letter since Lela always has so much information about the family and friends they have not seen in years. As she opens the letter, a second letter falls to the floor. The second letter is from Regina in Russia. As they read the letter, their joy turns to tears and anguish. As Lela had been the agreed upon contact person, at great personal risk, Regina has smuggled the letter out of Russia to Lela.

To My Beloved Family, especially Joseph & Anna,

My greatest regret in life is I did not get in the carriage and leave Saratov with you the morning you left. I was so naïve about life and the terrible people who had taken control of my Russia. When I went to see Igor Ivanson to secure Georg's freedom, he welcomed me like a long-lost friend. We talked of old times with my parents and how he and my father had been such good friends. I actually began to relax and feel like everything was going to be fine. He even had the servant bring in wine and cheese, and he came around his desk and joined me in the refreshments.

When I brought up the subject of releasing Georg, he became another person. With an evil grin, he told me he was planning on executing Georg at sunrise in the morning. I was so blind-sided; I was left speechless! All of a sudden, my whole world came crashing in around me. I could see in his face and by his demeanor that he knew I had no one to turn to and was enjoying every minute of my terror.

When I regained my voice, all that was left was to plead for Georg's life. When I offered him money or the brewery in exchange for Georg's life, he just laughed at my offer. He made it clear that the Communist government was taking the brewery and everything else the Karas owned. He only offered me one avenue to save Georg's life. Starting that night and for the rest of my life, I would be his concubine. He made it crystal clear that I could take or leave the offer. He gave me until sundown to make my decision.

I had two options. If I became his concubine, Georg would live out his natural life in prison, or I could walk out the door and be a lady on the street with no money and Georg would die at sunrise. As he recited my choices, he made it clear in an underlying tone that he was making me a benevolent offer because my father was his friend. Repeatedly, he gave me his word Georg would live if I agreed to his terms. Then he left me alone to decide if Georg lived or died the next day at sunrise.

I felt like I was drowning in a river with no chance of being rescued. There was absolutely no one to whom I could turn. When he left me alone, I knew I would not be allowed to leave the building even if I decided to walk out and leave Georg to die. I had walked into a prison I knew I would never be able to leave. The thought of having intimate relations with Igor Ivanson was unthinkable. I loved Georg; I was Georg's wife. How could I let that scum touch me? I realized I would have to consent to rape for the rest of my life. As I shook with sobs and screams, I realized how naïve I had been that morning. I should have been in the carriage with my beloved family. I know now, without a doubt, Georg would have chosen death rather than to have me forced into this situation, but that was no longer an option. At that moment, I would have welcomed my own death.

As I write this letter, I know Joseph hired a mercenary to free Georg and Alois. When Igor told me about the attempt, he laughed in my face. He said stupid Georg could have escaped but had stayed because he would not leave without me. I write this letter not only to inform the family about my situation but also to encourage another attempt to free the brothers. I can never leave Saratov. I must now live my life for my baby son and the baby I am expecting.

It is so bitter sweet. I conceived from Igor Ivanson almost immediately, like I never could with my beloved Georg. Now I can never leave even if the opportunity presents itself.

If this letter is intercepted by Igor, I will be killed, but I need to let my beloved family know my terrible fate. Also to let all of you know, I am now resigned to my life, and I will never leave Saratov. Igor has told me repeatedly that if I leave with his children, he will track me down to the ends of the earth. I know him as one of the most vindictive men who has ever lived, and I firmly believe he would carry out his threat. He is a powerful man. He has confessed to me he desired me from the first time he saw me when he visited in our home as my father's friend. His wife has never given him any children, so my children will probably be his only children, all the more reason we would never be successful in an escape. He is teaching our son to disrespect me, telling him often, "She is just a concubine." Sadly, I have to face the fact my son worships his father and would not leave with me.

Please, try again to free Georg and Alois, but I will never leave. I will love only Georg until my last breath. Georg needs to know I will never leave, so he can go on with his life if you can free him from prison.

Joseph and Anna, I love you both like sister and brother and dear Hettie and the twins as my own children. All of you will be in my thoughts and prayers for the rest of my life. I have such beautiful memories of the happy years I spent as Georg's wife and a member of the loving and respected Kara family. I now live with no love and no respect, and only my memories of better times keep me sane. Live a happy life for Georg and me. That will be your gift to us, the only thing you can do for me.

With regrets and resolve,

Regina Kara

For weeks, Joseph and Anna walk around in a daze like they are living in a nightmare. They keep thinking there has to be a way to free their beloved Regina from this horrible fate, but they both know Regina's resolve when she makes up her mind. They talk about her bittersweet fate. Regina now has the babies she always wanted but with a man she despises. They know she will never leave her children. Anna cries more tears than she thought she could shed. Regina is like her sister, mother, and best friend; she cannot imagine never seeing her again. Anna increases her level of activity, the only thing that helped her cope when she lost Max.

Without Anna's knowledge, Joseph again hires mercenaries to go back to Saratov to get his brothers. Months later when they return, it is again bittersweet news for Joseph to share with Anna. This time they were successful in sneaking a Jesuit monk's robe to Alois inside the prison. Wearing the robe, he walked out the front gate in full view of the guards, and then the mercenary helped smuggle Alois into Germany.

When approached with the idea of escaping, Georg was not interested in leaving even after hearing Regina wanted him to start a new life. The thought of life without Regina held no appeal. He has lived with the hopelessness of his situation for so long that he no longer cares about living or starting a new life with or without his beloved Regina. He has no energy; all day he sits in the corner and stares at the ceiling. Without his cooperation in an escape attempt, the mercenary told Joseph he felt the chance of success would be limited and the risk of both their deaths was great. It tears Joseph's heart out of his chest to hear Georg has given up on life. Joseph remembers how years ago their Uncle Wilmer became so melancholy and lethargic after the death of his wife that he withdrew into his own strange isolated world and never functioned in the real world again. Joseph wonders if that is the case with Georg.

The mercenary has a letter from Alois thanking Joseph for getting him out of prison. Joseph finds it ironic how in the letter Alois compared Georg's state of mind to Uncle Wilmar's condition. He feels Georg will never be able to escape the prison of his mind even if they can get him out of the actual prison. Alois knows that Georg found out Igor forced Regina into being his concubine and treats her badly, and there is not a thing he can do to save her. The hopelessness and injustice of the situation was more than he could handle, and his mind withdrew to a world of make believe. Alois said by the time he left the prison, Georg no longer recognized him as his brother.

As months go by, Anna finally accepts the fact Regina will never return; it is like she has died. Now Anna has friends around her all the time. Entertaining is like breathing, and she cannot be by herself since the memories are too painful. Joseph is glad Anna has her friends around to keep her mind off Regina and the twin they lost.

Chapter 9

At eight-years-old, Hettie is becoming quite a little performer and is featured on the piano at the country club and afternoon teas. Anna is so proud when she performs her beautiful classical music at her parties, but Anna also wants her to play a few of the happy new tunes of the day. Anna feels some of Hettie's music puts a somber tone to her parties; she wants happy and lively parties. Hettie absolutely refuses; she will play classical music or nothing. Other than this small disagreement, Hettie is a perfect child in her mother's eyes. Almost every day after school and practice, Hettie enjoys riding her pony with her two dogs following like shadows.

With his curly blond hair and deep blue eyes, Hans is so charming and handsome, and his delightful smile lights up the room. He is continually happy and sometimes a little bit of a rascal, but his mischief is always just for fun. He is a five-year-old delight. He especially enjoys when Anna dresses him up in the latest fashions and shows him off to her friends. He is the light of her life and her parties.

He loves to go to "work" with Joseph and learn how his father makes the beer. Joseph has a small, long-handled glass hidden especially for Hans to take a little taste of the brew before it becomes beer. It is a secret just between the two of them. Hans is such an easy-going, adventurous child with a light in his eye and a skip in his walk. Often, Joseph wonders how life would be if he would have two spirited little boys following him around, asking him questions and enjoying each other's company, but he knows he cannot dwell on what might have been. He has to focus on enjoying what he does have; he has so much more than Georg.

Anna is happy. Life is good again with beautiful children and lots of friends, who are always coming, going, or staying a few days. They also have a menagerie of pets in cages, pens, and roaming the property.

Lots of plans are made to celebrate Hans's 6th birthday, such a special day. In the morning, Anna and Hettie take Hans into Peking to have his picture made in his new white sailor suit. He is such an easy child to photograph; he loves the idea. After the pictures are taken, Joseph meets them for lunch at the club. In the afternoon, several of his little friends come for a party, and they stay for the night. Hans is so excited and happy. The children play all day and well into the night until they fall asleep exhausted. The next morning, they play until their mothers come to get the boys. Such a happy day!

Several weeks later, one of Anna's friends Sophia Hundsen comes to spend a few days with Anna and to conduct some business in Peking. The two ladies met years ago when Sophia lived in Peking. Now she lives on an island in the South China Sea area, but she returns often for long stays. Sophia always brings along her loveable little puppy Waldo. Everyone, especially Hans, loves the little ball of fluff. During her last visit, Hans and Waldo played from morning until night, and the puppy even slept with Hans.

Sophia arrives while Hans is at the brewery with Joseph. When Hans comes into the house, he runs to give Waldo a hug. Without warning, Waldo jumps up and bites Hans right above the eye. No one can believe the puppy has bitten Hans. They all think the puppy was startled from sleep and bit as a reaction. They tend to the blood running down Hans's face, and Anna sends for the doctor.

When the doctor arrives, he looks at the incident with a totally different view and orders them to put the dog in a cage. As the next few days progress, a nightmare unfolds. The happy little puppy turns into a mean, snarling, rabid dog. Because the bite is on the forehead, it does not take long for the initial symptoms of fever, headache, and general weakness to appear. Soon the symptoms progress into anxiety, confusion, hallucinations, increased saliva, and a tremendous fear of water. Within three weeks, Hans dies while restrained in a straight jacket. As he dies, Anna and Joseph cannot hold or kiss him. They can only watch the convulsions as he raves and snarls into complete madness. As he dies, Anna loses all hold on her sanity, and Joseph is not far behind. Hettie is spared the actual sight of Hans dying, but she can hear the sounds of his ravings and the horrible moans of everyone crying and wailing as they watch the terrible fate unfolding for precious gentle Hans. Hans Anton Kara dies at the age of six.

Now, both of the beautiful blue-eyed twins are dead!

Anton Kara and his daughter Martha

Laura &
Anton Kara

Alois, Regina, Joseph and Anna Kara (picture taken by Georg)

Georg, Joseph and Alios Kara

Five Star Brewery--Son-Ho-Shin Brewery in Peking

The Camel Train used for Beer Delivery

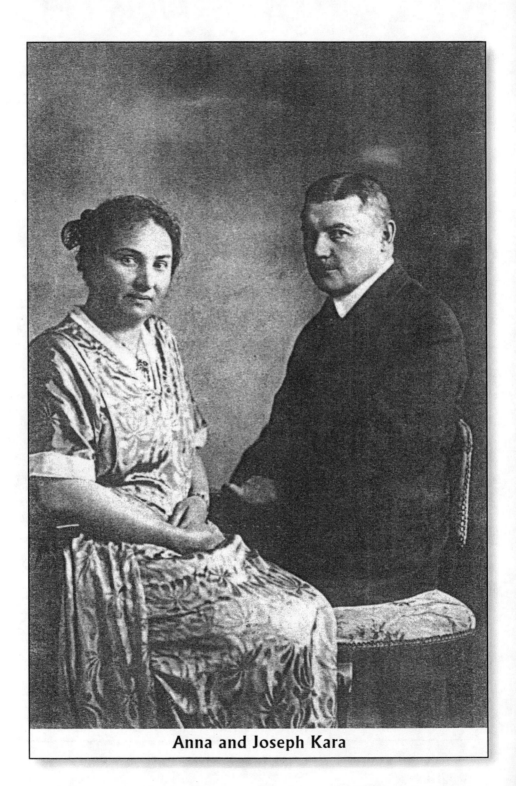

Anna and Joseph Kara

Hans Anton Kara
on 6th birthday

Vera Anna Kara

**Vera riding her donkey, and Hettie on her pony,
brewery wall and railroad tracks in background**

Aama, Vera and Hettie

Vera is representing a Czechoslovakian Bride with her two attendants for a multicultural program at the Rockefeller Center in Peking.

Hettie the concert pianist upon her return
from school in Europe

Vera Kara as a young woman

Several pictures of The Kara Family home near Peking

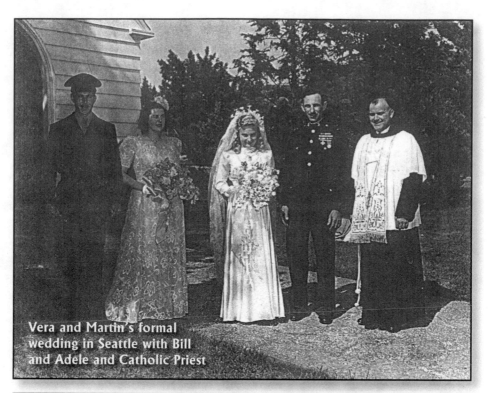

Vera and Martin's formal
wedding in Seattle with Bill
and Adele and Catholic Priest

Martin and Vera leaving their
wedding reception in Seattle
in his shiny black Hudson
Super Six Convertible

A house party at a friend's country home near Seattle

Will's first hamburger in Vera's kitchen

Will's arrival at San Francisco airport
from Prague via New York

Francis and Anton Friedel's wedding picture

Brewmaster Joseph at the Lone Star Brewery in San Antonio with the Brewmaster and assistant Brewmaster

In the story, Vera and Jack Jorg

Chapter 10

In the weeks and months after the funeral, Anna becomes obsessed with the fear some ill fate will befall her only living child. She hovers over Hettie, not letting her out of her sight. The distant lost look in Anna's eyes is like a knife in Joseph's heart, but he has no answers. Why has God taken both of the beautiful little boys? Seeing Hans' little friends laughing and playing everywhere they go is beyond terrible. Anna stays home and does not invite guests to come and stay. Joseph never liked the constant parade of friends, but now he would give a fortune to have them return and to see some sign of life in his devastated Anna.

Joseph comes up with the only solution he feels holds any hope for the future. He convinces Anna they should have another baby. He is saying baby, but she is hearing a boy or boys to replace the twins. As the pregnancy becomes a reality, Anna is filled with renewed hope and wants to share it with all her friends. She throws a party to celebrate and once again attends parties and social events. She throws herself into her usual constant activity, and Joseph treasures the return to a happier life.

When Anna begins to show the pregnancy, entertaining large groups at home becomes increasingly cumbersome, and since going to social affairs in a family way is socially unacceptable, Anna often invites a few friends to come to visit. During the last weeks of confinement, it is fashionable for ladies of means to check into the German Hospital in Peking. Anna can visit with the other ladies awaiting delivery, and when the weather permits, their favorite place to visit is in the rose garden in the courtyard.

One afternoon while sitting in the warm afternoon sun in the courtyard, Anna begins to recognize the same sensation she felt when her other three children were born. She stands up to go inside the hospital. As she is getting up, the baby starts coming out. The weight of the child begins to pull her undergarments down. She reaches up her skirt to grab hold of her underwear on the sides to ease the baby to the ground as she sits back down on the bench. She notices the baby is a girl. She shouts, "A girl! We've got a girl; we don't need another girl." As the squirming baby and the after birth reach the ground, Anna slips her feet free of her undergarments. She stands up, steps over the baby, and goes into the hospital. She never looks back at the child on the ground.

Anna's abandonment of the infant girl at her birth foreshadows the baby's future as fate will repeatedly heap adversity on her head, giving her one heartache after another without any love and support from her mother. Despite all the coming adversity, the child will grow up to be a vivacious, elegant, loving, caring and happy lady. She never has more then ten years of happiness at any one time before a devastating tragedy strikes the core of her life. Life will teach her how to land on her feet and make the most of what she has left, equipping her with a strong survival instinct that will help her thrive and bloom in difficult times.

As Anna enters the hospital, the staff notices the blood on her shoes, but she says nothing to them. They follow her to her room and learn the baby has been born. One nurse attends to Anna while another goes out into the courtyard and finds the baby crying and squirming on the ground. The baby girl is brought into the hospital and cleaned up. The staff presents the cleaned up baby to Anna. Anna tells them, "I don't want a girl; give her away." In China, the normal regard for a female child is such that the nurses take Anna's directive as a rational decision. They take the child to find a placement for her.

Later in the afternoon, Joseph and Hettie come to visit as they do almost every afternoon. When they don't find Anna in the courtyard, Joseph asks a passing nurse why Anna is not sitting and waiting as usual. The nurse replies, "Anna had the baby." With a big smile, Joseph hurries off to Anna's room.

When he gets in the room, he asks, "Where is our baby?"

Anna nonchalantly replies, "Oh, it was a girl, and I told them to give her away." Anna has not seen such anger in Joseph toward her since she mistreated Regina in Russia.

Through clenched teeth he says, "I don't care if it is a girl or a boy, I just want my child. How dare you give my daughter away!!" He leaves the room and demands the staff return the child. It takes some time, but they return the little girl. Knowing now how Joseph feels, Anna tries to make at least some half-hearted attempt to embrace the child, but Joseph can see the cold distant look has returned to Anna's eyes. He knows he has to find another to care for the child. He makes special arrangements, so the child will not be left alone with Anna. He tells the staff he just wants Anna to be able to regain her strength, and the child will disturb her rest. He names the child Vera Anna Kara; the day is May 23, 1921.

On the day Anna and the baby are to come home, the household staff swings into action as soon as Joseph and Hettie leave to get them. They decorate the house and prepare a big feast to celebrate the newborn. When the family returns, the spontaneous party is well received, especially by Joseph. Everything is light-hearted and happy. As the party gets underway, the staff takes the baby to change her diaper, and when they see the baby is a *girl*, the party comes to an abrupt end! The decorations are taken down, the food is put away, and everyone goes back to their usual task. Joseph is so dismayed to learn it is an insult to the parents if the birth of a daughter is celebrated. He tries to tell them it doesn't matter, but the staff loves Joseph and refuses to do anything to diminish him as a man. It appears Joseph and Hettie are the only ones happy about the chubby-cheeked, laughing little girl.

Joseph has hired a cheerful young single Chinese lady to come and live at their home to take care of the child. She becomes Vera's "Aama," pronounced like mama, and is the only real mother Vera ever knows as a child.

Anna hates the child and makes no attempt to hide the fact. Joseph tries to persuade Anna to try to love the child. She always says she will do better, but he never sees a change. Anna also makes some comments to Hettie in an attempt to turn Hettie against the child, but on this issue, Joseph stands his ground. Hettie has always worshipped her daddy, and pleasing him is important. He always spent a lot of time with her even when Hans was alive. He had always stressed to Hettie and Hans they should be each other's best friends, and now he expects her to be Vera's best friend.

Despite Anna's hate, Vera and Hettie have a warm and loving relationship. Together they enjoy and play with the menagerie of little animals on the property behind the brewery. The ponies are their favorites, and they ride them almost daily, sometimes for hours at a time. They have parrots, chickens, and all kind of birds. Vera especially loves the bigger dogs; her Great Pyrenees dog is big enough for her to ride.

Throughout her childhood, the punishments for Vera are severe and painful, from hard spankings to her mother's absolute favorite. She has Vera kneel in the corner on uncooked English peas for a mandated period of time. Her daddy has no power to stop Anna when it comes to mistreating Vera. He lays down the law, but in the end, all he can do is apologize to Vera. When he tries to intervene, Anna accuses him of spoiling her, and she treats everyone horribly for days. When Vera is on the English peas, the best he can do is come in the room and distract Anna. Then Vera can put her hands on the floor and relieve the pressure on the knees for short times. If Anna catches her, the time starts over. Vera and her daddy eventually develop a system that works without getting caught.

Vera spends her childhood riding her ponies, taking care of the little animals, or spending time at the brewery with her daddy, anything to stay out of her mother's sight. Joseph has a special little glass just for Vera. They keep the glass hidden. With the long-handled glass, she tastes the malt before it is mixed with the hops. It tastes really good, both sweet and rich. This is something only she and her daddy share, and it makes her feel so special and loved.

Joseph gets an occasional letter from Alois, who has immigrated to America. Each letter has a different postmark. He started out on the East coast and slowly migrated westward while he experiences the new country that he loves. This letter is from San Diego, and Alois has put down roots. He is married to a special lady, and they are expecting their first child. He sounds so happy. She is from a good solid family, and he loves working as a purchasing agent in his father-in-law's business. Joseph is so relieved that life is finally good and settled for Alois.

Joseph is so glad to have a permanent address to reply to Alois. In this letter as in every letter between the brothers for years, they lament over Georg's hopeless state. Now Joseph can share with Alois the letter they received from Russia forwarded again by Cousin Lela. Like the letter received many years ago, it is bitter sweet. The letter is only two short sentences in a familiar handwriting. It reads, "This letter is to let his beloved family know that Georg Wilhelm Kara has finally escaped from prison. He is walking the golden streets of heaven; he is free at last." It breaks Joseph's heart to hear his brother has died, but he has known for years death would be the only avenue of escape available to his beloved brother tortured in body and mind. Joseph can rest easier now that both his brothers are free and in much better places.

When Hettie is in school, Anna and Vera take many train trips by themselves, either to Europe, Prague, and the beaches on the North China Sea. On one trip, the train is held up by armed bandits, and they take all of Anna's jewels and money. On another trip to Europe, as their train pulls into a station, there is a vender selling apples outside their window. Vera begs her mother for an apple until Mama reluctantly agrees. They get off the train and buy the apple even though it is very expensive.

As they return to the train, a polite young well-dressed "government man" suggests they not return to their train car. He recommends they board the car behind it, the last car on the train. The mannerly young man climbs the stairs and opens the door to the car. When Mama notices the car has no other passengers, he says others will be coming on board at the next stop. As he closes the door, he tells Mama, "No matter what you hear, do not look out of this car." He is authoritative but so very friendly and genuinely pleasant that Anna does not get alarmed at what she could have considered an ominous comment. She simply smiles, nods her head in agreement, and thanks him for his help. The train leaves the station, and not far down the track, their car is disconnected from the train. They are terrified as the car starts to move backwards, rolling down hill until they reach the bottom of the hill. From the direction they had been traveling with the train, they hear loud noises, blood-curdling screams, repeated gun fire, and loud shouting. Then there is total silence. Anna heeds the young man's words; they do not look out of the train. (Maybe Mama Anna remembers another time when she had not followed a warning not to look out the carriage window in Siberia and the dire consequences.) They sit in that train car for two days before another train comes along. All they have to eat is the apple. Getting off the train to get the apple and following the young man's warnings undoubtedly saved their lives.

Joseph and Anna buy a beach house on the North China Sea at Fadahio Beach. Every summer, Anna takes Vera, Hettie, and some staff to the beach for weeks at a time. They play with the children of families in the other beach houses. Sometimes Joseph comes and stays a week or two, but mostly he comes for a day or two on weekends. Vera and Hettie love building castles and fishing with him.

One evening in Peking, Anna really likes the food as the family dines at a prestigious renowned restaurant. Joseph asks to talk to the head chef to compliment his food. They discover he is a Chinese chef specializing in Czech, German, and English foods. He calls himself Chef Franz. Joseph offers him more money than he is making at the restaurant to be their private chef. After he comes to cook for them, Anna's parties are even more special. Joseph does a lot of business with the different embassies inside the Legation, and Anna uses these connections to create her party guest list. It is a great combination for everyone. Even if she does not serve beer, the brewery reaps the benefits of her excellent parties. Because the elite of Peking come and enjoy Anna's parties at the brewery, the popularity of Five Star Beer continues to grow.

Hettie's love and talent for classical music is progressing. When she leaves for extended study in Europe, Anna is so proud of Hettie. Vera cannot play an instrument or sing. Occasionally, Vera is featured in programs at the Rockefeller Center in Peking. In one program, Vera is dressed up to represent Czechoslovakia in a multi-cultural program. Vera is a bride with two bridesmaids in attendance for the program. It will be one of the highlights of her life because she feels she has finally pleased her mother when she overhears Anna tell a friend in very glowing terms about Vera's performance.

Aama works to come up with ideas to help Vera gain her mother's affection. She dresses Vera up in the latest of fashion and pushes her into some of her mother's parties. For a few parties it works, and Anna smiles when Vera courtesies like a little angel. The ladies love her and compliment Anna on her beautiful daughter with the feisty attitude.

Both Hettie and Hans enjoyed being shown off to their mama's friends, but it gets under Vera's skin as she feels like a trained dog on display. One day before a party, Vera's mother is exceptionally unkind to Vera. That afternoon, as her mother introduces her at the party, Vera sticks out her tongue at the ladies and makes an ugly face as she courtesies so beautifully. Vera already knows she is headed straight to the English peas; however, she does not realize she will regret this action the rest of her life. Even when she broke the only valuable vase they had brought along from Russia, she did not incur as much wrath. Vera did not think it was possible to be treated any worse, but after the courtesy incident, Vera feels her mother never again looks directly at her or even acknowledges Vera's existence. Vera is now regarded by her mother as invisible, insignificant, or even a hired hand. The only time she acknowledges her presence is to punish her. Later in life Vera will realize she was such a rascal as a child because misbehaving became the only way she could get her mother's attention.

Every year on the morning of her birthday as Vera opens up the door of her bedroom, she is transported to a fairyland world. Her daddy has vases of roses all along the banisters and the stair railings leading downstairs. More roses are throughout the house. The sight and aroma is heavenly. He always has her favorite breakfast prepared on the breakfast table surrounded by roses. They spend the day together doing what ever she wants to do at home or in the city. It is always her day!

Vera attends the Catholic school in the Legation inside the wall. One morning as the chauffer is driving Vera to school, she sees an old Chinese man begging along the road. She instructs the driver to stop; she wants to share her tea with the beggar. Usually the driver would not stop, but he does not see a problem with complying with the eight-year-old girl's request. She gives the old beggar a cup of tea. He is so appreciative, and Vera feels so good. She has done something for someone less fortunate than herself.

That afternoon as they are returning from school, they are met in the same stretch of road by a very large angry Chinese mob. They want to take Vera out and kill her. They are calling her a "White Witch." The driver and Vera finally understand. After drinking her tea, the beggar died! It is all the driver can do to get Vera home safely.

True to Anna's usual hateful attitude toward Vera, when they get home, she is irate with Vera for being so utterly stupid. How could she have given a worthless beggar the time of day, much less to stop the car? Joseph is just thankful Vera is safe and rewards the driver for getting her out of the terrible situation. Joseph has to pay a large sum of money to settle the incident with the beggar's family.

Besides her daddy, Vera has no one to talk to since Hettie is away at school. She wonders if she really killed the poor beggar. Vera's Aama takes her in her arms and sooths the frantic child. At the time, her Aama, a quiet unpretentious young woman, probably does not realize the infinite wisdom she is sharing with the child; she uses the incident to teach Vera valuable life long lessons. First of all, she assures Vera that her intention was so pure and she should always be proud of stopping and giving the poor man the only thing she could have given him at the moment. She also assures Vera the cup of tea was a memorable last event in the man's life. She makes it clear that the tea did not kill him. He was just old and was probably going to die soon anyway. Perhaps his family saw she had given him the tea, and when he died, they saw a way to get money from the rich family. She also tells Vera as a fact of life with the low regard of the elderly in her country, it can also be the family of the old beggar saw her kind gesture and killed him to get money from her father.

Aama helps Vera understand that all we can do in our lives is the best we understand at the moment. If it all turns sour, as this situation has for everyone involved, she will just have to pick up the pieces of what is left and make the best of a bad situation. She needs to know that the people who love her understand, and the others do not matter. She has to rise above the situation and know she did the best she could have done for the beggar. So many times in her life, Vera has to do exactly as Aama recommended in this horrible situation. Cry over the loss, back off to evaluate, and then carry on with what is left.

Throughout her young life, one of the things that brings the biggest punishments for Vera is when Anna catches Vera speaking Chinese. Lots of time is spent on the English peas because of this infraction. Vera never understands why her mother does not realize she spends more time with Aama and her Chinese friends speaking Chinese than she does with her own family.

After years of hard work, Joseph has enough money to pay off his two partners, Tam and Mr. Cho, and Joseph becomes the sole owner of the Five Star Brewery. It has been a good partnership, and after all these years, they are all still good friends. The venture has been successful, enjoyable, and profitable for all involved. It's another excuse for Anna to throw a big party. To commemorate the occasion, the brewery develops a mug with a glass bottom with a picture of a beautiful woman on the bottom. A saying develops, "When the woman gets dim, it is time to quit drinking."

At the end of the semester, a prim and polished Hettie returns from Europe an accomplished classical pianist. She is accompanied by her new boyfriend, Avery. Everyone except Anna and Hettie can see he is just a rounder and womanizer. He knows just what to say in every situation, especially to the women. Joseph can see he has no intention of working for a living and has absolutely no money management skills. He is just like a loveable worthless stray, and the longer he stays, the more they all come to overlook his shortcomings and to accept him as a lush. When he proposes, Mama and Hettie are overjoyed. Anna throws her complete attention to planning the biggest and best wedding Peking will see in years. The guest list reads like the who's who of Peking. The up-coming wedding is top line news on the social page and the talk at every ladies group for months. All six of Hettie's best friends are to be bridesmaids. Hettie also has to find four of the groomsmen to escort her friends as her fiancé will only have two friends coming from London for the wedding. Anna and Hettie are having the time of their lives planning the wedding and the pre-wedding celebrations.

Hettie's wedding dress is a beautiful, elegant creation designed by the most expensive designer in Peking. Hettie's absolutely beautiful in her wedding gown at the last fitting three weeks before her wedding. Hettie is not feeling well at the fitting, but everyone is sure it is just fatigue from all the pre-wedding celebrations. Within the week, she becomes sicker and sicker. It is Scarlet Fever! At the age of 24, two weeks before her scheduled wedding day, they bury their beloved Heidwecka Anna Kara in her wedding dress.

The family is devastated. Vera has lost her best friend and a kindred spirit. Joseph has lost his beloved Hettie. Although he was able to save her through hell and high water during their treacherous move to China, he now cannot do a thing to save her. Anna is never to recover; life has just dealt her too many blows. Without any other source to blame, she blames Vera. She tells Vera often she should have died instead of talented Hettie. What does she have to offer the world? Nothing, and yet she lives and Hettie is in the cold ground.

As usual, Aama is again the only person eight-year-old Vera has to turn to in her own sorrow of losing Hettie. Joseph is in his own world of grief, and where Vera is concerned, Anna is a raving lunatic. Aama helps Vera understand she did nothing wrong. She needs to cry for her loss, pick up the pieces, and then carry on with her life. She needs to enjoy life to the fullest as Hettie would have wanted for her. She also helps Vera feel compassion for her mother. She helps her understand how much her mother loved her sister, the twins, and Regina, and now they are all gone. She tells Vera it is not right for her to treat Vera unkindly, but she is a woman full of pain. Vera begins to understand and learns to say, "Mama is just so disappointed."

One day Anna was having an afternoon ladies party out on the veranda. Vera went into the party preparation area and tried some of the pineapple punch that was being served. She liked the taste and had some more, never realizing it was heavily spiked. Vera became drunk. When Anna found her in this condition, she blamed Aama for not watching Vera closely enough and for encouraging her to be around when Anna was having her parties. Anna fired Aama. No matter how Vera pleaded and cried, it was final. Aama was gone. Before she left, Aama tried to explain to Vera that her mother was so full of hate that it was controlling her life and spilling over into Vera's life. She told Vera to let things slide off her back in her life and to be like a buoy in the ocean, letting the storms of life blow over but never letting hate control her thoughts. She told her hate is like a contagious disease that destroys the person who hates and spills over into the lives of those around them. She told Vera to forgive, to forget the hurt, and to move on with her own life. Otherwise, she will become just like her mother, full of hate. Always be happy, look for the good in your life, and always try to make people around you happier because you are in their lives. Choose to be happy, and you will be the one to reap the benefits. Just like that, Aama is gone. Vera will never see or hear from her again. It is like she has lost her mother, and it is her own fault. Vera cries as much or more for Aama than she has for Hettie. She does not know how she will face life without Aama to lean on and talk to about problems. She decides to take Aama's words of wisdom to heart to repay the woman for her years of love and service.

The next years are not good for Vera as Anna unleashes her full fury of punishments on Vera at every opportunity. Vera learns how to make a life of her own with her loving father, friends she made among the Chinese staff, her friends at school, and the animals around the brewery.

Chapter 11

After Hettie's death, the family skips several summers before they resume their usual retreat to the beach. The first return trip is difficult for everyone. Vera is so glad to be at the beach with her old friends, so she can escape from Anna's continual worship of Hettie's memory. Vera misses Hettie terribly, but Anna is stuck in the past. With Anna's gloomy attitude, neighbors do not come to visit but once, which in turn makes Anna even more irritable. It is not a good summer at the beach.

As she grows up, others notice Vera's ability to speak many languages with ease and proper pronunciation. She can speak in Czech, German, or Chinese on any subject without hesitation. A philanthropist notices her unique talent and offers to send her to several classes in Europe and pay the tuition for her to attend the American High School in the Legation in Peking. Vera and her family feel it is a great honor and graciously accept his offer. For the first three years of high school, she devotes herself to studying and to making good grades. Vera is barely five feet tall, and she tries to make up for her height by excelling in everything she does. During school days, she has to be careful to get to her driver before the gate closes so she can go home and study. Only once did she miss her driver and have to go to Mr. Cho's house to be "put under" for the night. During her senior year, she starts to have some fun, goes to parties, and stays over night with friends.

When Vera graduates valedictorian of her senior class and fluent in five languages, even Anna has to admit it is an accomplishment. Vera can speak her three mother tongues (after all, Chinese is the tongue of the only real mother she has ever known), and she has added French and English. For graduation, her daddy Joseph gives her a big party at the Peking Hotel. She invites all her friends; Vera is in charge of the guest list, not Anna. Vera never once says her parents gave her the big graduation party. She remembers, "Daddy gave me a big graduation party at the fanciest hotel in all of Peking."

Joseph begins to see the same crazy ideas that led to the downfall of individual freedoms in Russia taking hold here in China. The dissenters are talking the average-to-poor Chinese citizen into believing private ownership of property is wrong. Joseph starts sending large amounts of his money to Switzerland, New York, and back to Prague. He hopes to avoid some of the same problems he had when his money was declared worthless after they were forced out of Russia and to protect his money from being confiscated by the new government. His only mistake is allowing Anna's mama, who in the past has shown a severe lack of money management skills, to sign on the account in Prague.

During this time Joseph hides the Chinese emperor's nephew in the brewery to protect him from public persecution and possible death. The emperor shows his gratitude by giving Joseph a gigantic six by eight foot wall tapestry made with gold threads. It was from the Qing Dynasty circa 1644. Vera calls it the "Birds of Paradise" because it contains two storks in the woven scene. The top inscription contains Mandarin characters saying, "For the use of the emperor."

The emperor loves Five Star Beer. When he comes to the brewery, it is always a big event. All the Kara's personal staff members are replaced by staff the emperor brings along. Anna is especially in awe when he comes because she likes royalty and titles; after all, her mother and father had titles. Joseph and the emperor are good friends, and Vera remembers going to the Summer Palace as a child.

Once, the emperor's men came by themselves to pick up beer, and one of the soldiers gets so drunk he rides his horse up the front stairs of the house. Those front stairs come up from two sides to the first landing of the house, and from that landing, the stairs continue up to the main level of the house. The horse makes it up to the landing and makes it unscathed down the steps on the other side. The soldier is severely punished as the horse could have broken its legs. However, it is unusual for anyone to get that drunk at the brewery.

After high school, Vera attends Peking University. At a party at a friend's house, she meets a young man named Wally Wagner from Tientsin. He is such fun; everyone loves him.

Wally and Vera have so much in common and can talk for hours. Wally is the funniest man she has ever met, always the life of the party; his quick wit is razor sharp.

Wally's father is a German engineer hired by the Chinese government to build bridges. They pay him with land instead of money. Some of the land had iron ore, so he brought in experts to set up a mining operation. He has become a wealthy man, and he and his family are living the good life, working and playing. Wally's family has race horses. To take their horses, family, and friends to races all over China, his dad has bought a C47 twin piston engine transport, the biggest transport airplane available. They have such fun on their trips to the races.

Despite Wally's flamboyant personality and gift of gab, usually the mark of a "never do well," Wally is an exceptionally industrious man. He and Joseph hit it off instantly, but Anna hates him from the first time she hears Vera likes him. She hates him almost as much as she hates Vera because he is not royalty. Even though she detests Vera, only royalty is good enough for her daughter.

Wally and Vera ride horses whenever they can break away from school. Sometimes they ride the horses at the brewery, but often they go to his father's estate and ride the well-trained horses. Vera loves that her father likes Wally. The fact that Anna hates him makes him more attractive to Vera.

Joseph offers Wally a summer job at the brewery. Joseph starts him out as a work hand, but he plans on making him his assistant. The young man is intelligent and willing to learn. His light-hearted attitude and funny stories make work fun. He is also willing to do any kind of work, which is unusual for a young man with his money. He also understands how to make the most of his money, an important trait to Joseph.

The U.S. Marines guarding the U.S. Embassy in Peking enjoy drinking Joseph's Five Star Beer. Martin Friedel, a Lieutenant from Texas, comes to the brewery often to procure a supply for special occasions on the base. The quantity he buys makes him a good customer. He is handsome, full of energy, and never meets a stranger. Martin and Wally get along from their first meeting. Joseph especially loves when the two of them are in the same room; there is laughter and lightheartedness. When Joseph finds out Martin grew up in Texas speaking Czech with his immigrant parents, he takes him to the house to meet Anna. Anna loves him. He is so much fun; they speak Czech fluently to one another. He is debonair in his immaculately pressed U.S. Marine uniform and a real gentleman. During their conversations, they discover Martin's father and his uncle had been students of Anna's brother Frank Czerny, a professor at the University of Moravia. He is in tight with Anna.

Wally and Vera fall deeply in love. They are best friends; Vera has never been so happy. They get married despite Anna's objections, but with Papa Joseph's blessings. They are married at St Joseph's Catholic Church. They have a sit-down dinner for 200 at the Peking Hotel with monastery drinks, champagne, and a dance. After a wedding trip, they live at the brewery. The house is so big they can avoid Mama. Vera learned from little on how to avoid Anna in the house, and she teaches Wally to do the same.

Wally and his father are getting worried about the repatriation situation. Because of all the hateful things Hitler and the Nazis did during the war, there is a fear and distrust of Germans worldwide. Germans living in other countries are being forced back to Germany, especially if they never got citizenship in their new countries. Wally's parents are German, and his mother went back to Germany for Wally's birth so that he would be a German citizen. At the time, it was a good thing, but now they realize it was a terrible mistake. Neither Wally nor his daddy ever agreed with or supported Hitler, but now they are reaping the whirlwind his hatefulness created. Joseph and Anna are becoming concerned for Vera and the baby she is expecting. They might be drawn into the repatriation because they are married. They start to talk to Wally and Vera about getting a divorce "on paper" or a "friendly divorce." In retrospect, Vera feels strongly her father really was concerned for her and the baby's safety, but Anna was trying to get rid of Wally. She wants Vera to get interested in Martin.

The beautiful little boy Will Hans Wagner is born on August 15th at the much enlarged German Hospital where Vera had been born twenty years before. Will has beautiful blue eyes and three strands of blond hair. Vera is a small woman, and the baby is nine pounds. Unlike her mother, Vera has severe labor pains.

Anna is the best grandmother. The problem is she does not see herself as the grandmother. After Hettie's death, Anna never really regained her grasp of reality. In her borderline insanity, she is slowly claiming Will as her own, at least in her own mind.

Will is only two months old when Wally gets the order; he is to be repatriated to Germany. Joseph and Anna talk Wally and Vera into the "friendly divorce," so she will not be forced to go with Wally or be summoned later. Vera and Wally spend their last weekend at the beach house at Fadahio Beach. They love each other so deeply that it is tearing out their hearts to say good-bye. They pledge their undying love to one another and promise to wait until eternity for each other.

Wally is placed in a cattle car along with many others and taken to the seashore. There are five ships waiting to take the repatriated Germans back to Germany. Wally is in the lead ship flanked by the other four ships. Only days later, Vera gets a telegram telling her that the lead ship Wally was on hit a mine and sank. No survivors.

She has been a wife a little over a year and now is a widow. Joseph and Wally's father help her through the agony of losing her loving husband, best friend, and the father of her little boy. Anna is quietly overjoyed since she hated Wally and now might have a better chance to claim little Will. Vera cries until there are no more tears to find, picks up the pieces of her life for her son, and carries on as best she can with a broken heart.

Chapter 12

When Martin gets the news of Wally's death, he comes to the brewery to give his condolences to the family. Martin, an honorable man, had been friends with Wally and befriends his widow, caring for her as a brother would. She is so blown away by Wally's death, and her little boy needs a man to play with him. What starts out as a casual acquaintance and support for Vera soon grows into a relationship. Martin is ten years older than Vera, but in height, she only comes up to his chest. They grow to love spending time together. It is not the rollicking, adventuresome times she had with Wally, but Vera loves the respect and understanding Martin always shows for her grief. He never pushes her; he knows she needs time to heal.

Anna likes him and invites him to the house as often as she can find an excuse. Joseph likes Martin because he brings some of the same sunshine Wally always brought to the brewery.

Months later, when Martin takes Vera dancing at the officers' club, she really starts to take notice. He is a dream on the dance floor. The big band sound is all the rage, and Martin loves to waltz. She can remember hiding on the balcony at the country club as a child and watching the couples waltz around the dance floor below. The women were floating in their big skirted white dresses, and now she is floating around the dance floor with a dream of a dancer. At the officers' club, she notices how his friends smile their approval as they dance. She can see he is a very loved and respected Marine. They make a beautiful couple.

Times in the world are changing everywhere, especially here in Peking as the Communists gain tremendous power.

Rumors are flying that the U.S. forces are going to withdraw. Martin and Vera's budding romance is thrown into a tail spin; things are moving so fast.

Joseph again makes plans to leave everything he has worked for behind. He and Anna can return to Austria and take Will with them as their child. Joseph would like to go to America and join Alois, but Anna insists they go back home to Prague. Vera is an adult Chinese citizen and cannot go with them, so she will have to stay. Vera meets the thought of leaving with mixed emotions. She loves China, the only home she has known, and she loves the Chinese people and their way of life here in Peking. However, she can see everything is changing.

Through the years, Anna has amassed a huge collection of exquisite art, intricately carved ivory statues, and carved wood chests. Anna also has many unique pieces of furniture to display her collections. Joseph comes up with a plan to save her treasures.

Joseph takes all of Anna's best chests, the tapestry from the emperor, the ivory statues, and furniture and packs them all up in huge crates he and his workers built.

Martin receives his transfer papers back to the states. He proposes to Vera, and she accepts. He promises her he will be able to get her to America. They are married by the base chaplain; it will be easier to get her out of China as his wife. They will have the formal wedding and consummation when she arrives in America. He does not want to take the chance of leaving her behind pregnant because he knows she is already raising one child without a father. Now that Vera and Martin are married, Joseph gets Anna's beautiful chests out of the crates, and they fill them with Vera's extensive wardrobe and put them back in the crates.

Joseph continues with his plan. He ships the boxes of Anna's collection to Martin's family's home in Robsville, Texas.

If Vera never gets to America, he would rather Martin have the treasures than the Communists. In Russia, the Communists seized all their family heirlooms, and he will not allow that to happen again.

Martin applies for papers to get Vera out of China and then to America. He spends hours and hours on telephone calls, talks, and trips to see the people who can help him get her out. A desperate situation is developing since he has to get her out before the Communists take over. If he fails, she will be branded as a traitor for wanting to leave.

When Martin leaves with his platoon, Vera prays desperately for his plan to work. The Communists outside the wall come in and take over the brewery, and Joseph becomes no more than a hired hand in his own brewery. Joseph gives Vera Anna's jewelry. He knows from experience that she can use them as money if worse comes to worst. Within days, Joseph and Anna leave for Prague, and they take Will with them. Vera knows because her mother loves Will she will be good to him. Vera has a good friend living inside the wall. Her mother was Chinese and her father German. She had been married to a German man, and they had also gotten a "friendly divorce." Vera enjoys staying with Jane, but she is terrified the officials will want information about her parents.

In the last week, almost the last day, before 350,000 Communists march through the North Gate, Martin gets the papers for Vera to leave China. She flies to Shanghai. There she boards a small ship full of people in the same situation. She is assigned to a bunk in a room with rows of bunks. In the bunk above Vera's bed is a seasick young lady throwing up all over Vera in the bottom bunk. Vera recalls, "It was just like being outside in rain. Sometimes it came slowly, sometimes it poured, but it always stunk. Everything came down but the girl. The vomit stuck to my body, hair, clothes, and the bedding. It was like sleeping in a pig pen." Finally, they reach Hawaii. While they go ashore, their accommodations are cleaned. Vera and her friends from the ship have such a fun time touring the island while the ship is in dock. She wishes she could stay longer since Hawaii is so beautiful and the people are so friendly and laid-back.

As she gets to know the others on the voyage, she learns they will soon be with their families in America. Only Vera is going to marry a man she barely knows in a completely different culture and country. She sometimes suspects Martin also lives on a very different social-economic level. In spite of their different backgrounds, he is a good man, and she loves him. She believes they will have fun and have a good life, but she misses her son and family.

Chapter 13

When Vera arrives in Seattle, Martin cannot meet her because he is on duty. He sends a couple, his best friend and his wife, to meet her and to take her to his apartment. They welcome her so warmly; Bill and Adele become lifelong friends. When Martin arrives, it is like they had never been apart. She knew he was handsome, but with his pressed uniform and the look of love in his eyes, she thinks she has never seen anything better. After their hellos, the first thing Vera asks Martin is, "Where is your staff?" It never occurred to her that there is no staff! Back in Peking, Vera never cared for her self, never even drew her own bath. Now she has to learn how to do everything. Martin gives her his apartment, and he stays on base until their formal church wedding.

Their military wedding is beautiful with all the handsome men in their dress uniforms and their beautiful traditions and manners. Vera feels such love and acceptance from all his many friends in the Marines. They leave the wedding with the top down in his black Hudson Super Six convertible with streamers flowing and cans clattering.

Martin is such an understanding and fun man to love. He loves showing her new things in America and helps her learn how to cook and to keep house. Vera has such unrealistic expectations for the meals. The first time she tries to make French fries, she takes a ruler and cuts each piece of potato to exactly the same length. The table has to be set just to perfection; nothing in the house can be out of order. That is how everything was in their home in China. Anna demanded perfection from the staff, and Vera thought everything had to be perfect. These unrealistic expectations make for some hard times for Vera. Slowly she accepts Martin's view that the best you can do is all you can do. Vera tries so hard; she learns how to do many things very well in a short time. Martin brags to everyone about her ability. He encourages Vera to lose her accent. With her usual ability with language, she quickly learns how to talk Texan with the long drawl like he talks. Whenever she says something he thinks does not sound right, he gently brings it to her attention by quietly saying, "Hey, what are you doing?" Anyone overhearing his comment does not even know he is referring to her word pronunciation.

Growing up, she only watched Aama cook, and all the recipes she brought along are Chinese. Many days she makes several trips up a steep hill to the little corner grocery store several blocks away. In the morning, after Martin leaves, she gets out her recipes and makes a list of ingredients she will need. She walks up the steep hill to the store in high heels. Because of her short stature, Vera always wears very high heels to appear taller. Many times the store does not have all, and sometimes almost none, of the ingredients she needs, so she has to go back down the hill to find a new recipe and repeat the trips until she has the ingredients for a full meal. Martin is always so complimentary on any success he can find. When the meal does not turn out as expected, he suggests they go for a ride in his convertible. They usually end up at a drive in for a hamburger, his absolutely favorite food. She learns to make hamburgers, one of her first successes.

Martin spends hours shining his beautiful black Hudson convertible, his pride and joy. He insists Vera learn to drive. He is ever so patient with her, spending hours driving on vacant parking lots on the base. It is a standard shift, so they hop around a lot until she can start off smoothly. One day she turns a corner too short and puts a dent in the fender; Martin is not a happy man! Even then, he is a real sport and forgives her in short order. He makes her continue until she is an excellent driver with a license.

During the first few months of their marriage, Martin spends hours in communications with Vera's father and the authorities in Prague to get Will back with his mother. Martin promises her he will get her son back, and he never gives up. Vera knows her mother is attached to Will, but he is her little boy. He is almost the exact age Hans was when he died. Vera is torn between wanting her son and not wanting to hurt her parents. Joseph is living in hell trying to do what he knows is right even though he would love to keep Will almost as much as Anna. Martin is vehement about it; Vera has the right to raise her own son. Even though the paperwork with the authorities is endless, and there are roadblocks at every turn, Martin does not take no for an answer. His tenacity is how he finally got Vera out of China, and he will work until he gets Will with his mother. Then Martin is reassigned to San Francisco, so some of the paperwork has to be started over. Martin adopts Will, so he can get him to America. They never tell Will about the adoption. Martin had been around Will as a father figure before they left China. He was only a few months old when Wally left for repatriation in Germany, so Will never knew his real dad.

On every furlough or leave, Martin and Vera go to Robsville, Texas, to visit Martin's mom and dad, Anton and Francis Friedel. The first time they arrive to visit, there sitting in the front yard are the big crates with all of Mama and Daddy Kara's treasures, waiting to be uncrated. The huge crates sitting in the Friedel's front yard spark community interest in Martin's new bride. Because of the Chinese connection, mystery and intrigue surround the gossip. Family and friends who love Martin are concerned Vera will not be good to or for him because she was raised in such a different culture, and people tend to distrust people and situations that are different.

Vera and Martin's parents get along from the first meeting. She speaks their language. As a young man in Slovakia, Martin's dad Anton had been in the military but wanted to see the world. He loved adventure and making money; his goal was to be a wealthy man. He got into a scrap of some kind, and he was given the choice to leave Slovakia or go to jail. The decision was not hard. He landed on Ellis Island and lived in New York City. As a boy, he had been raised in the country, so he does not like city life. He traveled around the U.S. until he came to South Texas.

Through his travels, he learns English. He gets a job as a clean-up man in a bar for a Spanish man; they get along well. Anton learns some Spanish and how to bartend and to serve people. He saves his money and soon buys a bar just outside the gates of the Navel Air Station in Corpus Christi. It is a good move since the soldiers always stop in for a beer when they go on leave and when they return. Sometimes the bar is their destination.

He marries Alice, and she helps him in the bar. The babies start coming. They have four children just like stair steps. They have a house, but the children are practically raised in the back room at the bar. Even though Anton Friedel is a harsh, blunt taskmaster, they are a happy little family. The children learn to help out with what ever needs to be done. At the birth of the 5th child, Alice dies in childbirth. Anton is left with five children under eight-years-old, no wife, and a very successful bar to run. Alice's parents and family help. They take turns keeping the children especially on weekends when the bar is full.

It isn't long before Anton meets Francis Hermis, a young Czech lady from Robsville, which is north of Corpus Christi and miles from the bar. As Anton can speak Czech and is quite a ladies' man, he sweeps her off her feet. She has had very few men pay her any attention. Even though she is a lovely intelligent young lady with a happy disposition, she is on the verge of being labeled an "Old Maid." She is head over heels in love with her new boyfriend, Anton. Being he is Czech and obviously has money, her parents are also swept up in the infatuation. In short order, he asks her to marry him. The traditional huge Czech wedding is planned. They sew the wedding and bridesmaids dresses, rent the hall, hire the band, order the beer, line up the cooks, the whole nine yards. After all, Francis's parents are very wealthy, so their only daughter's wedding is going to be an affair to remember.

The wedding day comes, and low and behold, bridegroom Anton drives up with his five children. He has never mentioned the children to his lovely bride-to-be. Anton, the scoundrel, has played his cards right. He knows neither Francis nor her parents can back out with all the guests already starting to arrive. They are trapped by the situation. Sure, Francis can call off the wedding, but she and her parents know after this, no respectable young man will ever call on Francis. In the Czech and German cultures, once a girl is engaged, she is considered to be used material. She will be like a divorced woman, and divorce is totally unacceptable. The wedding goes on as scheduled.

Francis is not cut out to raise a family in the back room of a bar. She will endure it for a time, but her father expects Anton to change the living arrangements as soon as possible. He gives Francis a 300 acre black-land farm with a seven-bedroom house near Robsville. Her father makes sure the property is *only* in his daughter's name. Anton likes making money and works hard to learn how to make the property prosperous. He sells the bar and puts his attention to farming. He appreciates that Francis is good to his children. With the proceeds from the bar, he buys several office buildings with good long-term business renters, like the U.S. Post office and such. He is a hard worker and becomes a successful businessman and farmer.

Martin is the only child born to the union, so the farm will be his some day. Anton is a strict disciplinarian; he deals out severe punishments for not immediately carrying out his orders. Martin remembers the time his dad told him to do something and he did not comply. His dad threw a hatchet at the boy, and it stuck in the wall near Martin's head. Martin learned quickly to follow his father's orders.

Anton had been a soldier, and he demands Martin go into the military. He thinks the Marines are the toughest, so he enlists Martin in the Marines at 17. For Martin, the strict discipline in the Marines is like being at home. A natural leader, he advances quickly. Getting out from under his daddy's thumb is a relief, for it allows Martin to enjoy life and to develop his more laid back, loving attitude like his Grandpa Hermis.

As a youngster, Martin and his family went to lots of Czech weddings with the barbeque, beer, and four-hour dances to round out the evening. The children learn how to dance at an early age. Parents and extended family always take time to teach the youngsters to dance. As Martin grows into a young man, he finds he has exceptional ability on the dance floor. He especially loves the waltz. When he whirls and twirls on the dance floor, it is like being on air. The ladies love dancing with him. It is such fun to see his partner's face light up with smiles when he twirls her around under his arm and brings her back into his arms to continue to whirl and twirl. Soon everyone in the hall is watching. The dances are always over too soon.

Even though his life at home as a child was not easy, as a grown man, Martin is drawn back to the farm. His brothers and sisters often visit with their children. His daddy is sometimes a hard man, but his kids all know he loves them. Martin is especially close to his mother, and he loves farming. He helps his dad as much as he can when they are home on leave. While Francis loves the new daughter-in-law, Anton can not believe his good fortune. She can speak fluent Czech! The young ladies from Czech families in the area can speak Czech, but not like Vera.

For both Vera and Martin, the absolutely best part of being home on leave is going to dances. They try to schedule their leaves when weddings and anniversaries in the family are planned. At the first dance, Vera wins everyone's hearts. Martin, tall and handsome in his uniform, is so proud of his new bride. They make such a beautiful couple. With her high heels, she carries herself with such grace and confidence, and her clothes are exceptionally beautiful. Anyone can see she is from money, but she is so pleasant and never puts on any airs like she is better. As she talks to people, she makes them feel like they are the most interesting people she has ever met. At the dance and throughout her life time, ladies often ask where she buys her clothes. Vera breaks out in a big smile, momentarily reminiscing. "Oh, I brought them along from China." Occasionally she buys something new and fashionable just for fun, but her lifelong wardrobe is centered around the clothes she brought from China. Luckily, she never changes size. Her personal seamstress in China had made such fabulous classic garments in just the right colors and design to accentuate Vera's tiny body to perfection.

Vera cannot believe the primitive living conditions in the Friedel home. No indoor plumbing, no running water (well, sort of running water). When you need water, you run to the cistern in the yard, fill a bucket, and run back in the house with the full bucket. There is a washroom off the kitchen with a portable bathtub, but first the bather has to get the water and then heat some on the stove while carrying in the rest of the water for the bath. When the bath is over, two people grab the tub by handles on each end, pick it up, carry it out, and dump the water off the porch. Martin makes sure he is there to help carry the water in and out for Vera's bath. Spring and fall are comfortable and enjoyable in the house with a refreshing breeze coming through the open windows and up the stair well. However, in the heat of summer, Vera remembers being upstairs and sweating. She recalls, "We weren't perspiring; we were sweating like animals! I went down to take a cold bath to find some relief; I felt better in the tub. But I was always 'sweating' again by the time I got back to the second floor. No need to dry, a person was always perspiring unless it was winter, then ya froze."

In winter, there is only heat in the kitchen and the parent's bedroom. That room is also used as the sitting room in winter. No one heats a living room in the winter except on Christmas Eve. Vera and Martin's bedroom is up the flight of cold stairs to a freezing bedroom. Mama Friedel always has a warm feather bed and flannel sheets on the bed. She also makes sure there is a warmed brick wrapped in a cloth under the covers for Vera to put her feet against when she crawls into the freezing bed. This special attention always makes Vera feel so special, loved, and appreciated.

There isn't any gravel on the road leading to the house from the public road. During rainy weather, the car is left at the road, and everyone walks to and from the house barefooted. With no running water, there is no easy way to clean up when they get to the house. In warm weather, they sit on the porch until the mud dries on the feet. Then when the leg is moved, the black-land dirt that has dried will fall off. Finally, a pan of water is used to wash the feet before entering the house. In winter, they scrape off the main mud and go inside to stand or sit around the wood heater in the kitchen until the mud dries and can be knocked off into a pile before the feet are washed. Keeping a relatively clean house in rainy weather is a constant battle.

The living conditions are hard for Vera to get used to, but she loves Martin's mom. Francis is always so good to Vera. She always wanted a daughter and treats Vera as her own child. She is so much better to Vera than her own mother. Vera makes the best of the situation; she loves to visit the farm at every opportunity. Vera even loves Anton with his cocky, Czech, macho attitude. She talks Czech with both of them, and it makes the place feel like home.

She misses her folks, especially her dad and Will. They write often, but that is not the same. Her mother's letters are like getting poison because they are trying to get Will to the U.S. Mama tells Vera so many hateful things that finally Martin decides he will not let Vera read her letters. He just tells her any important information from the letter. Vera always treasures the letters from her beloved father even though, occasionally, he makes mention how hard it is going to be to lose Will. Vera knows and understands his pain since it is the same pain she feels without her precious boy. Vera learns she can always share her pain with Martin's mom. Francis attentively listens and helps Vera feel better about her need to raise Will herself.

Joseph writes Vera how hard it is living in Czechoslovakia under the Communist rule. He is having a hard time keeping his money in Switzerland; they are always coming up with new laws to get more of his money. When they arrived from China, they lived in the boarding house he had provided for Anna's mama. He bought the apartment house for her mother right after he married Anna when her mother gambled away the family castle and became destitute. Anna's sister Marie never married and also lives there. Joseph always kept the property in his name and laments how he should have remembered that lesson, especially when he sent his money out of China for safe keeping. When they first arrive in Prague, he discovers Anna's mother has gambled away a good part of the money. In hind sight, he knows he should never have trusted her with signing privileges.

Each letter is full of details of the big villa he is building for Anna. He bought the land and is building the villa in Vera's name. It is the only way he can be sure it will not be taken by the Communists since Vera is an American citizen now.

He relates that Anna was livid when she found out they will be allowed to live in only a small portion of the new villa. They will have to rent the rest to other families. She cannot have servants, so now Marie is filling the role of servant since Anna has no intention of doing the work. Vera is secretly thankful for the distance between her and her mother.

Chapter 14

Finally, all the paper work is finished, and Martin makes all the arrangements for Will to fly by himself on a commercial airline from Prague to New York. There he will change planes and continue on to San Francisco.

Although it is like losing another child, Anna finally accepts he is leaving. She takes a heavy wool blanket to her seamstress to make a new suit for Will. It is long pants, a vest, a coat, and a matching hat. The handsome suit is quite appropriate for the weather when he leaves Prague, but it is like being in an oven by the time he gets to San Francisco.

The stewardesses treat Will like a little king. Six-year-old Will speaks no English, only German and Czech, and he is painfully shy and reticent. The crew coaxes him to take off the heavy coat and vest, but he refuses. His "mama" (Anna) told him he could not take off the coat until he is with his mama in San Francisco.

Looking back on the trip, he understands why they tried so hard to get him to take off the coat. Everyone else is in short sleeves, some even in shorts. They give him chewing gum, but he had never had any and swallows the first pieces. He asks for another package and swallows all those pieces. When he asks for another package, the stewardess asks what he has done with the other gum. Through pantomime he motions that he has swallowed them. With more hand motions, they explain he needs to chew it until it loses the flavor and then throw it away. They all have a good laugh when he understands and enjoys chewing the last pack for a long time.

Martin and Vera meet him at the airport, and everything goes smoothly through customs. The pictures show Martin as happy as Vera to have their son with them. They take pictures while Will enjoys his first hamburger in Vera's kitchen. They have such fun showing Will all the new things Martin had shown Vera when she arrived in America. Martin is such a good father, so Vera does not see any reason to mention Wally. What good will it do for Will or Martin to bring up a father Will never knew?

Will loves the farm in Robsville. Grandma Friedel is such a good cook and makes him feel so special. At his age, he never notices the lack of human comforts in the house. He has such fun playing with all the farmyard animals and just running free all day long. He comes in the house only to eat and to sleep.

When Martin's first baby is on the way, the entire family is overjoyed. Martin and Vera always make sure Will is part of the celebration of the baby they are expecting. He is as excited about the baby as Martin's folks, especially Francis, who is thrilled to welcome her first grandchild.

Vera gets a letter from her father that Anna's mother Amalia has died of complications after she broke her hip in a fall. Vera remembers her grandmother from their frequent visits back to Prague with her mother when she was a little girl. She remembers her as a fancy dresser but a lady of few words. Her Aunt Marie always made young Vera's visits fun. They would take walking trips to see all kinds of special things, so they could get out of the house together.

On every return trip to San Francisco, they take some more of Joseph and Anna's treasures along, but when Martin gets the order he is being assigned to Korea, they must put all their belonging in storage. Vera and Will move in with Mama and Papa Friedel. Will starts school in Robsville just before Christmas. He can speak very little English, so he fails the first grade. That summer he learns English, and the next year he passes easily. It seems Will is adjusting nicely to life in America.

One day, Vera gets a telegram, informing her Martin is missing in action! It only says Martin had been on a clean-up mission in Korea with his men. The telegram does not give any more information. Vera, Will, Francis, and Anton wait for information. Vera cannot believe she may be a widow again, especially while she is with child; surely fate will not be that cruel again.

A month later, she gets another telegram. Martin has been found and will be returning state side to the hospital in Corpus Christi. When he gets back, he tells them his troop had gotten stranded and had no supplies for weeks. He and his men had to eat whatever they could find. The experience leaves Martin with multiple health problems, and he spends months in the hospital.

About the time he gets better and is released from the hospital, he is reassigned to Camp Lejeune in North Carolina. Construction of the base between Wilmington and Moorehead City had been started in 1941, so everything is almost brand new. The base is beautiful with big trees, a long beachfront and exceptional housing for the families of the Marines. Their house has a large living room and a spacious yard filled with trees. Unless he is in school or asleep, Will spends every hour playing with their menagerie of little animals or climbing trees in the back yard.

Vera is happy and content in their new home. The letters from her family in Prague are her only cause for concern. Her daddy writes that living with Anna after Will left is like living with a stranger. She is so unpleasant to Joseph, blaming him for allowing Will to leave. She treats Marie like a hired hand. Vera and Martin start talking about bringing them to America.

They can help Daddy with Mama, but what will they do with dear, sweet Marie? She will not want to come, yet they cannot leave her there by herself.

One sunny afternoon, the phone rings, and Vera answers, expecting the call to be from Martin telling her when he will be home for the evening meal. It is Wally! Alive and well!

There she stands pregnant with Martin's child, talking to her beloved Wally, her first love, first husband, and the father of her son. Wally has spent forever trying to find her. He tells her how the mix-up occurred when she was notified he was dead. He had been in the lead ship of the five-ship fleet. As they entered a heavily mined area, the captain of the second ship contacted the captain of the lead ship. He thought he knew the locations of the mines better, so the ships changed places. Evidently, he did not know as much as he thought. His ship was blown to smithereens and sank; all aboard that ship perished almost instantly. He was not on that lead ship that sank. He only learned yesterday from his Uncle Ernst that he had been reported dead on that ship!

Wally shares that when he got to Germany, he escaped. When he made it to Switzerland, he had no money, but he sent a telegram to his father to send him money. He does not understand why his father never sent the money, but Vera can tell him. His father had shown her the telegram. The telegram was from Switzerland, and his father was convinced no German could get out of Germany. Also, Wally had signed the request for money with his Christian name, Walter. Because he had signed it with a name Wally never used, his father had been further convinced it was just someone wanting to get money, a cruel hoax to extort money. Oh, if only they would have known it was really Wally!

In the phone call, he tells her he had been in three prisons and escaped from them all. He also tells her he found out yesterday his father had been repatriated to Germany and had died in prison. Vera thinks he does not know she is remarried. He wants to know about his son. He tells her how getting back to them was the only thing that brought him through all the prisons and terrible situations.

He says the trans-Atlantic call is costing him a fortune, and he will call her back in a couple of days when he gets more money. He is so happy to hear her beautiful voice. He hangs up.

The minute Martin sees Vera's stricken condition, he runs to her side and asks, "Has someone died?"

Like a person in a trance, she replies, "No! Someone is alive!" Then in a tiny voice just a little more than a whisper, Vera says, "Wally is alive; I just talked to him on the phone!" Martin is speechless!

They are concerned for their baby with Vera in such turmoil. Martin takes a couple of days of sick leave to be with Vera, but he is at a loss for a workable solution since any decision is going to leave lives destroyed. Martin had known Wally just a short time but liked him. How awful for Wally to return to nothing. But, they have a good life here in America, and he loves Vera and Will.

After a few days of thinking of all the options, Vera knows when Wally calls again, it will be the worst day of her life. If she was not pregnant with Martin's child, the solution would be simple, but she is pregnant and must consider the welfare of her unborn child! It would not be fair to Martin; he has never been anything but a model husband and father. On the other hand, Wally was also a good husband and father. With the new baby on the way, she knows what she has to tell Wally about her new life. She keeps repeating, "He is saving money to pay for a phone call to hear the worst news a good man can ever hear."

When the call comes, Vera is stronger than she expects. She tells Wally she has remarried. He says he really already knew since her name is not Wagner any more. She tells him Martin is so good to them. Wally said he remembers him and knows he is a kind and honorable man. Vera tells Wally how good Martin is to Will and that they have never told Will he was adopted by Martin. Vera tells him she is expecting Martin's first child. At this point, Wally tells her his telephone time is up again. He promises to call again after he has some time to think.

The next time Wally calls, he tells Vera he will stay out of their lives. He knows it would be confusing for Will if he appears and tries to be a father. He said he will call occasionally just to hear about his son and how things are going for him. Vera thanks him for being so understanding, more understanding than any good man should ever have to. Life has dealt them a bad hand. They will both have to cry, pick up the pieces, and then make a good life out of what they have left. Wally tells her in post-war Germany, he is living from hand to mouth, and he cannot provide as good a life for Will as he has with her. He tells her he will love her until the day he dies. She says she loves him; she is so sorry things have turned out so terribly for them. Wally hangs up, and Vera does not hear from him for years.

A few months later, the baby comes, a healthy baby girl. They name her Joan Francis after Vera's parents Joseph and Anna and Martin's mother Francis, but they call her Joanie. Together, Will and Martin play with Joanie like she is a little doll. With Martin as a role model and because of the eight-year difference in their ages, Will's interactions with Joanie resemble an exceptionally close father-daughter relationship more than a brother-sister relationship. This proves to be of paramount importance as life unfolds.

While they are living in North Carolina, Martin's daddy dies, and Francis is devastated. It is decided Will will live with her for a while to help her adjust. Will does not mind since he always loved staying at the farm. He will miss the baby and his family. He and Grandma quickly become a team. Anton Jr. "Tony," Martin's brother, finishes the crop for the year and rents the land for the next year.

During this time, Joseph writes how difficult taking care of Anna has become as Marie's health is beginning to fail. Martin writes Joseph with a special invitation for them to come to America to visit Vera and the family. He invites them to stay permanently if they like it in America.

Joseph writes back, thanking them for the invitation, but Marie will not and really cannot make the trip. So, he will just have to make the best of their situation.

Will lives with Grandma Friedel for three years. The only money they have to live on is the rent check from Martin's brother for the crop land. Will rides the school bus to school in Robsville. He remembers the light bulb suspended in the middle of the rooms with a pull chain to turn the light on and off. They have a lot of animals to take care of each day. They plant a huge garden and can or freeze all the extra vegetables for use when the garden is out of season. They work all the time, but they laugh and talk while they work. They have a radio and a crank telephone on the wall, but they do not have a car as Francis does not know how to drive. A neighbor comes by on Saturday to take them to town to get grocery staples and some animal feed. The same neighbor comes back on Sunday and takes them to church. Otherwise, they never go anywhere. Each week they get two newspapers: the Sunday paper with the funnies and a Czech paper Will cannot read. He and Grandma talk mostly Czech. Vera and Will write each other often, his only life line to the outside world besides school. Will remembers going barefoot to the mail box at the county road in the summer to get and to send the letters. The extreme South Texas heat has the road so hot it is like walking on coals. He always runs as fast as he can so his feet will not be on the ground for long. He loves living with his grandmother, but he misses having friends in the evenings and weekends. He is lonesome, and the work is hard and continual.

Before long, Martin is reassigned to Corpus Christi. They move into a brand new home in a new sub-division. The postage stamp sized yard does not have a sprig of grass. The house is new and nice but not as nice as the house in North Carolina. Vera is expecting again. Martin Jr. is born soon after they arrived in Corpus Christi. Will is still at the farm with Grandma. He can be at both houses, but the base housing is on the other side of Corpus Christi, so he would have to change schools. Vera and the babies visit at the farm often; Francis and Will love playing with and holding the baby. Joanie is quite a handful, and Will's youthful energy is useful to follow her around to keep her out of trouble. Martin's health begins to fail and after an extended stay in the hospital, he is given early retirement from the Marines. They all move to the farm, and for the first few months before his retirement takes effect, Martin commutes to the base from Robsville. He plans on planting and harvesting the entire crop himself with Will's help.

Martin has the road from the house to the county road graveled for an all-weather road. He takes great pride in his vehicles and having them full of mud is not acceptable. His pride and joy is his new green Hudson Super Wasp four-door sedan with all the little windows down the side with a factory installed musical trombone horn under the hood. He also adds a set of longhorn bull horns on the hood. On his way home from the base, about a mile from the farm, he engages the musical trombones. The sound is so melodious and happy echoing in the distance through the trees, letting everyone know he is on his way home. What a happy sound!

Shortly after they move to the farm, Grandma Friedel gets sick and dies. Her death leaves such a big hole in their lives; she was such a quiet dynamo. She had been an awesome grandma to Will and all the grandchildren, but Will also loved her as a best friend. They had lived alone together on the farm for so many years. Vera loved her as a caring mother and her confidant, and she had always been Martin's rock.

After Francis dies, Will is invaluable to Martin and Vera. He knows how everything on the farm works and can help Martin with the field work. Martin and Will have two bumper crops. They are a really good team, but as Martin gets sicker, Will has to carry the load.

The family goes dancing as often as there is a dance anywhere in the area. They take the children along just like the other families. They take a big pallet along, so when the kids get tired, they go to sleep. Except for Martin's health, life is good. They work hard all week long, but when the weekend comes, they dress up and have a good time with their many friends. On Sunday morning, no matter how late they stay up the night before, they go to church to worship and to visit with church friends.

Occasionally during the week, the younger children bring friends home after school to spend the night. They are also farm children, so they understand there are chores to be done each day after school. The friends join in to get the work done quickly, so they can play. Will has too many chores to have friends come home after school; he is everyone's rock, a big assignment for a little boy.

Vera is an exceptionally good cook, and everyone enjoys showing off her culinary delights to their friends. Many weekends if there isn't a dance, they have a family or two over for supper. They play games until all hours of the morning. The children always hate Saturday mornings. All the Chinese treasures have to be dusted, a monumental, tedious, and boring weekly task.

Vera's father writes Marie has died, so now they are free to come and visit. Joseph writes he will have his business in order in Prague just in case they decide to stay. He will leave Lela's son Heinrich in charge of renting and maintaining the villa. The apartment house had been confiscated by the government when they moved into the villa. He says again how good it is he put the villa in Vera's name and mentions his regrets he had never managed to get the apartment house in her name.

With each passing month, Vera can see Martin's health is deteriorating. He is diagnosed with lung cancer, probably a result of his ordeal in Korea and the pack of Camels he smoked every day. Now she knows for sure having her mother staying in the house will be difficult. She looks forward to seeing them but dreads dealing with her mother on a daily basis in the same house. Despite her fears, they are coming, and she must deal with it.

When they arrive, Vera is so disappointed in her father's demeanor. He is a broken man. The last time she saw him, he was still a take charge, get things done man. Life has dealt him too many blows. He is now an old man. While he is still the man she knew, he is no longer able to rise above adversity. She is so glad they have come to live with her. Joseph helps where he can with the children, but he cannot drive since he always had a driver. Instead, he stays with the children while she drives Martin to the doctors and gets supplies at the commissary. Mama, on the other hand, thinks Vera and her children are the servants. She expects them to take care of her every need. Martin is the only one that can straighten her out. He is so smooth that she does not even get angry with him when he demands she treat them better.

It is especially poignant for Vera to have her mother here in the house where Francis had treated her so tenderly and lovingly. She wishes she could wave a magic wand to turn Anna into Francis. Joseph and Vera slowly develop a routine, so Anna spends a lot of time in the big wooden swing under the huge oak in the front yard. That way she is out from under Vera's feet and out of her hair. Vera can do her work without continual interruptions with Anna's demands for attention or her usual hateful, demeaning comments. The two eventually find a way to coexist peacefully.

To add to her woes, Vera discovers she is expecting again.

The first month the Karas are in America, Martin tells them he wants to take them to San Antonio to see the city. He does not tell anyone he has made special arrangements with the Lone Star Brewery in San Antonio. Joseph will be the special guest of the brewmaster. They spend all afternoon at the brewery. The head brewmaster himself and his assistant show Joseph all around the facility. They treat him like a visiting dignitary with special introductions in very department throughout the brewery. After they leave the brewery, Vera notices a new spring in Joseph's step. His demeanor is more like the father she always knew, a man proud of his accomplishments.

Life is so good, but Martin's health is deteriorating rapidly. As he is planting the third year crop, Vera looks out the window several times and sees Martin hanging over the side of the tractor, vomiting and still plowing. At 14, Will does farm work way into the night to help Martin plant and cultivate the crop. He does not mind; it is just what he needs to do to help his sick dad and to keep the family going. He just cannot have a life of his own. Thankfully, Uncle Tony comes to help when he has time.

One Saturday afternoon as Will and Uncle Tony are enjoying a snack in the kitchen, just laughing and talking. Uncle Tony tells Will he has been thinking about adopting a little boy. He tells Will, "Then we can have the same kind of great relationship you and Martin have had since he adopted you." Will cannot believe his ears. Tony does not know Will had not been told, and he feels horrible for exposing the family's secret. He asks Will not to tell anyone he told him.

Will is so hurt and confused, but he does not say anything to anyone. He mulls it over in his mind for days. He reflects back on all the years growing up with Martin as his father. Even with this new perspective, he cannot think of any incident where he was treated any differently than the other children. Will never tells Martin he knows. Martin has always treated him as his son. What good will it do to tell him now when he is so sick?

As Martin gets weaker and weaker, they cannot dance every dance at the socials, but they stay the entire evening and enjoy visiting with friends. Soon they are leaving before the dance is over. When he said he is not going to any more dances, Vera knows the end is getting near.

Martin and Vera's third child is born; they name him Ronald Martin Friedel and call him Ronnie. He is born in the midst of Martin's illness, a difficult time for everyone, especially Vera.

At the age of 42, Martin Anton Friedel dies at the Naval Air Station Hospital in Corpus Christi. After only 10 happy years of marriage, his death leaves Vera with a broken heart, four children, one just two months old, and a 300 acre black-land farm.

Vera is glad Will, her father, and Uncle Tony can help her with the decisions. They decide to rent the land to Louie Rychetsky. Just living there on the farm is going to be enough work to keep Will, Joanie, and Martin Jr. busy. Will knows how to plant the garden and Papa Kara helps him. Vera, Joanie, and Junior plant the seeds and help gather the vegetables. They hang another swing under a tree near the garden, so Anna can sit and watch the others work. The rent from the land is their only source of income. Although life is hard, Vera does what she always does. She backs off and evaluates the situation, picks up the pieces, and then makes a good life for herself and the children out of what she has left.

Chapter 15

Will is now the father figure for the family, and all the manly responsibilities land on his young shoulders. He has always had that kind of relationship with Joanie even when Martin was alive, but baby Ronnie will never know any father figure but Will.

Vera throws herself into taking care of the family. When the weekend comes, she longs to have somewhere to go to be around people, but she has noticed a strange change in their friends, especially the women. Even at church, they are not friendly. She and Martin had always had such warm and loving relationships with so many people. Now they are cold and getting colder to her. She does not understand; she needs them more now then ever.

She gets a long sympathy letter from Bill and Adele, the couple they were friends with in Seattle. When Vera answers their letter, she mentions how people are not friendly any more. When Adele answers her letter, she tries to explain a sad but real situation. Vera is now a threat to the women's marriages. She is beautiful, outgoing, full of fun, and now "single." She is no longer a wife; she is now a rich (land rich) single widow. Vera cannot believe what she is reading, but it explains everything. She knows Adele is right; now she knows why the husbands will not talk to her and even avoid looking at her if at all possible.

Lieutenant Gib Gibson, one of Martin's good Marine friends, finds out Vera is not receiving Martin's benefits and helps her until she gets Martin's benefits and his insurance proceeds. Martin's Hudson holds so many memories, so Gib helps her trade it in on a new red station wagon. They put the bull horns on the new car, but the musical trombone horns stay in the Hudson. It is just too hard to hear the melodious sounds of the horns, knowing Martin is not just around the corner coming home.

Will graduates from high school in Robsville and joins the Air Force. He has always wanted to fly, and the recruiter says he will get into flight school. Vera and the three children are so sad to see him leave. He has always been there to take care of them, but they are so glad he is going to get to fulfill his life's dream.

Vera is lonely, so she takes a part time job at the county library. The money barely covers the babysitter, but she needs to be with people. She works harder when she gets home to keep up with all her work. At the library, many people are strangers, so they are friendly like her friends used to be. She begins to notice there is one gentleman in the library almost every time she works. He likes to make small talk as he checks out his books. Soon Arthur Bruno talks to her as he comes in and as he leaves; he always makes her feel so good. One of the other workers mentions to Vera she never saw him in the library before Vera started working. She tells Vera he is a ladies' man; most people do not like or trust him. The friend knows he and his wife have never gotten along. His wife is from a wealthy family, and everyone knows they do not like him. They make sure he does not get his hands on any family money; they keep everything in corporations and trusts. Instead of giving her a warning, the information leaves Vera feeling sorry for him.

Vera starts to look forward to talking to Arthur. They talk off and on for months. When he finds out she likes to dance, he suggests they meet at the little watering hole not far from the library. She knows she should not, but she is so starved for some fun that she stops on her way home. As soon as she walks through the door, she knows she does not belong. She and

Arthur dance only one dance, and she goes home. She knows full well she should not have stopped, especially considering she is driving the red station wagon with the horns on the hood. The next day, she cannot believe how many people saw her car at the bar.

It isn't long before Arthur tells Vera he and his wife are getting a divorce. He tells her how he has been unhappy for so long until he met her. He has been waiting for her all his life, and he is not going to take the chance of losing her. In her vulnerable state, she believes every word. Martin's brothers, her father, and Will cannot convince her not to date him. He has no job, and while he likes to act like he is in real estate, his sales never work out. Most people know him to be a dishonest man and will not do business with him. The more people tell her he is a loser, the more she is drawn to him.

If she thought people were cool to her before, now they are downright rude to her. Arthur and his wife never got along, but now Vera is the other woman, a home wrecker! In a small town, it does not take long before the wagging tongues slash her good reputation to shreds.

Vera calls Gil, and he helps her buy another less-noticeable new car. She decides she might as well have some fun and enjoy some of the terrible things they are accusing her of doing. She and Arthur start going out to clubs, having a high old time with Vera picking up the tabs. As soon as his divorce is final, they are married by the Justice of the Peace. She had been alone for five years and feels it is time to have fun and to enjoy herself.

Arthur wants Vera to meet his family; his parents and his married brother and sister's families live near Fort Worth in Blair, Texas. The family welcomes Vera and her children like they are long lost kin. Vera really likes his family. His siblings are all successful business people and large ranchers. She gets the general idea that Arthur has been the black sheep of the family. She can tell they are all so glad to meet her, hoping she will be good for him. His first wife would never have anything to do with his family; she never came to visit. Vera thinks she missed a lovely family experience. Arthur is so attentive to Vera when they are visiting with his family.

Arthur is not interested in farming. He likes expensive race horses, fine cars, and fast women. Vera was living the life of a fast woman for a little while, at least until they got married. As soon as they tie the knot, Arthur starts talking about a huge place for sale on the river near San Marcos, Texas. He talks about it all the time, and he wants to show it to Vera. He often tells her the farm with all the work can be sold. Then they can move to the ranch with lots of money to live on. On the ranch the family can have fun riding horses, driving four wheelers, and playing in the river. He knows how much Vera enjoys riding horses.

The family loads up in her new car to take a look at the 530 acre horse ranch he has in mind. The ownership of the horses will convey to the buyer with the property and stay on the ranch. The entire ranch is completely awesome. The land slopes down to the river surrounded by massive oaks with limbs touching the ground. The house is grand, not fancy but a typical sprawling West Texas ranch home with a big porch facing the river. The river is beautiful as it meanders along the edge of the ranch. The ranch has so many types of land. A lot of the land has lush green grass intertwined with trees and fenced for horses. Several places leading to the river are deep gorges with cave like recesses perfect for exploring. The children are so excited to think they can live in this beautiful place.

Arthur finds a buyer for the Friedel family farm. Vera is feeling guilty about selling the farm, but she feels she and Arthur need a new start so that they can make a go of their marriage. There are too many memories in the old house.

She signs on the line to sell the farm, and *they* buy the ranch together. Under Texas law, the farm had been Vera's separate inherited property in which Arthur had no ownership, but the horse ranch now is community property owned equally by both husband and wife.

They are so happy, riding and playing on the ranch. The house is big enough for Joseph and Anna to have a private room and bath on the other side of the house. Anna really likes the ranch; she and Joseph take long walks along the river and through the woods. Vera notices Anna's health is slipping, but Vera is in a world all her own with all the beautiful horses. She rides often during the day when the kids are in school. She remembers the time she and her sister Hettie spent riding horses back in China. She notices Arthur is leaving more and more. He continually tells her she is not living up to his expectations of a wife. He does not like her cooking or how she keeps the house. He especially does not like all that Chinese junk she has all over the house. Vera withdraws to the horses and the animals on the ranch where she feels accepted.

Will comes home on leave several times. He and the children all have so much fun exploring the caves and ravines on the ranch and playing in the river. They are all so glad to be together again.

Vera buys Arthur a fine new red pick up truck with lots of chrome and loud pipes. For the biggest part of the first year, the ranch is so much fun for the children. Arthur loses no time in teaching the children how to do all the work, grooming the horses and feeding them. At first he works with the kids, but soon he does less and less of the work. Soon the children have no time to ride just for pleasure. Work is all the kids have time to do both before and after school. Still Arthur is always angry that they have not done enough. In the evenings, he disappears into town and does not come home until late. Vera wants to go, but he can always find a reason she needs to stay home. In the mornings, he sleeps until almost noon; then he piddles with a few chores until the kids come home from school. He tells them all the things they need to get done and then disappears into town. Everyone is glad when he leaves.

The only time the whole family is happy together is when they go to visit Arthur's parents in Blair. Arthur is like his old self, paying attention to Vera and being kind to the children instead of being angry all the time.

On Will's next leave, he brings home his new girlfriend, Elaine. Everyone loves her. It is like she has always been part of the family. She loves to laugh and has a laugh that just makes everyone around her want to laugh and be happy. She and Vera have a very easy relationship; they enjoy each other's company.

Anna is beginning to walk off into the woods, so they have an alarm installed on the doors of their living quarters. Joseph hires a young Spanish girl Angela to help with Anna; he is tired of Anna treating Vera like a hired hand. He can see Arthur is destroying her self-confidence, and Vera does not need her mother also belittling her. Angela's husband Manuel is soon a full-time employee at the ranch with Joseph paying the wages. With Manuel's help, the children can relax a little after school. Arthur thinks the hired help is a waste of money. Vera and Joseph tell him if they cannot keep the help, Arthur will have to stay home and help with the work. He never complains about the hired help again.

After Vera and Angela feed the children and get them off to school, Vera makes breakfast for her folks. She serves it in the sitting room near their bedroom, so Anna can not roam while she and Joseph eat breakfast. Anna usually sleeps late. Vera is pretty sure she just does not like eating with the "help." Joseph and Vera look forward to their time alone together.

They linger over the last cup of coffee before she goes for her morning ride.

Throughout their lives, it was usually Joseph apologizing for Anna's treatment of Vera, but lately, it is Vera apologizing to Joseph that she did not listen to him about Arthur. She starts to compare Arthur to Hettie's boyfriend, Avery. She talks about how everyone but Hettie and Mama could see he was worthless. Vera laughs because she has been just as blinded by Arthur's smooth talk. She often says how Hettie was better off dead; she never had to face the fact she was such a bad judge of character. She never had to face the "I told you so" from her family. Papa reminds her that Arthur came into her life when she was reeling from Martin's death. She was extremely vulnerable, and Arthur had taken advantage of her situation. Vera always treasures how her father can make her feel better.

One morning Papa is not waiting for breakfast at the table. She finds him sitting next to their bed. He is holding Anna's cold hand; she died quietly during the night. Vera can see in his eyes that his reason for living has just slipped away. Vera meets her mother's death with such mixed emotions. Now she knows for sure she will never get her mother's approval. Some how she had always felt before she died her mother would take her in her arms and tell her she loves her, but now that will never happen. Somewhere in the depth of her being, she feels a quiet release for an unfulfilled need; it is a sad but liberating realization. They bury Anna Kara in the Catholic Church Cemetery in San Marcos.

Joseph still takes long walks along the river, but now he walks like an old man. Vera and the children rally around Papa Kara to help him over Anna's death. He has always been such a pleasant man with such good stories to tell. They love listening to the stories around the table after supper. Sometimes he repeats the same story, but the repeated story will usually have some extra detail of interest. For months the family falls into a happy life style with lots of laughter around the house and evening meals.

As summer turns into fall, all of a sudden, Arthur does not go into town in the afternoon. He has Vera go into town and buy a big combination lock to put on the front gate until they can get an electronic keypad gate installed. Every time some one comes driving down the drive way, Vera notices Arthur steps out of sight until he is sure he knows the visitor. Now he is always angry. He hates Joseph's stories and belittles Papa when he repeats a story. It is not long before Joseph does not come out of his bedroom. The kids sneak into his room to hear his stories, but soon Arthur comes looking for them and wants them working.

They start going to Blair every other weekend. Again like before, when they are visiting his family, Arthur is a really nice guy. He starts talking about selling the ranch and moving to Blair. Vera thinks it might be a good thing. He never tells her what happened, but she knows Arthur has made some powerful enemies in San Marcos. Vera has been raised Catholic and making her marriage work is always of paramount importance. She feels they might have a chance to work things out with his family around.

The children are heartbroken, and Joseph is devastated at the thought of leaving Anna's grave. Every day Manuel takes Joseph to visit Anna's grave, and he spends the time just sitting on the bench talking to her grave. When the first strong norther[*] of the winter comes, Joseph catches a really bad cold, and it is not long before it develops into pneumonia. Vera takes him to the hospital, but he has no will to live. As Joseph dies, Vera holds

---

[*] norther (in the U.S. Gulf coast region) a cold gale from the north

her beloved father in her arms, telling him how much she loves him. She knows she is losing her best friend and her source of strength. At the age of 90, Joseph Anton Kara is buried next to his beloved Anna in San Marcos, Texas.

Chapter 16

Arthur finds a large cattle ranch near Blair to buy. The beautiful horse ranch on the banks of the San Marcos River is sold, and they move during the Christmas holidays. When the children start school, they discover how well respected Arthur's family is in the area. They are treated special like they had been treated in Robsville before Martin died. Arthur's siblings know people who can be hired to run the ranch, so the children have time to be involved in extra curricular activities in high school. Life is good again. Arthur looks like he is really interested in making a go of their life and the cattle ranch.

As the newness wears off, he starts to disappear every evening again. Vera knows he has found a new friend; she finds tidbits in his pockets and pick-up truck. He has her convinced it is because she is such a sorry wife. With no Papa alive to tell her differently, she believes Arthur's lies.

Arthur's cousin is a dynamite lawyer. Arthur hires him to file for divorce against Vera. Vera hires the only lawyer she feels she can afford, and they go to court. As the divorce hearing unfolds in the court room, the judge mentions that in addition to getting half of everything, Arthur is asking for alimony. Vera is dumbfounded, and Vera's attorney is surprised. Her lawyer has no idea what is in the papers. The divorce is granted. As she is leaving the court room, Arthur made a huge tactical mistake. With a smug evil grin on his face, he begins to taunt Vera, telling her how stupid she has always been. He tells her he had planned this all along. He tells her he divorced his first wife to get Vera's money. It is not a smart move on his part because when her mad takes over, Vera wakes up from her down trodden state of mind. She decides she is not going to allow this gigolo to walk off with the Kara and Friedel money and to laugh at her on top of it.

That very afternoon she hires a new lawyer, the most expensive in town. He wastes no time in getting a petition for a new trial approved. He stresses to Vera that possession is 9/10th of the law. He helps her make arrangements to sell the cattle. Three large double-decked trailer truck loads of cattle are taken to Fort Worth Stock yards and sold. The money is put in the "deep freeze." Arthur had moved a lot of the big tractors and heavy farming equipment to his father's ranch to use them there and never brought them back home. The lawyer helps Vera find haulers, and they go and pick up all the equipment. At first Arthur's father objects, but when the drivers tell him the equipment is really Vera's, he has to agree. He steps back and lets them take it all.

When they go back to court, it is a totally different trial. Vera's lawyer is in charge. He shows the judge the money has come from Vera's father and Martin's family and his life insurance. He calls a witness who heard Arthur tell Vera after the first hearing how he married her to get her money. Then Vera's lawyer calls Arthur to the stand. Her lawyer asks him only a few questions, and then the judge starts asking Arthur the questions. *How has he earned money in the time they have been married?* Arthur had to admit he never held any job. *Who bought you the fine pick-up truck you drive?* Vera. *Who pays for your expensive clothes?* Vera. *How much money did you bring into the marriage?* Arthur admits he had not gotten any money from his first divorce; everything belonged to his first wife's family.

The judge rules he should leave this marriage with just what he brought into the marriage: nothing! Vera tells her lawyer she will buy Arthur an old truck, so he can leave and never bother

her again. After the trial, Arthur's lawyer, his cousin, comes to Vera and apologizes for the first trial. He said he should have known better than to believe Arthur. He suggests Vera and her children stay in the area because Arthur's parents genuinely love the children and want them to be in their lives. Vera and her children have no other family, so she welcomes the offer.

Like usual, Vera picks up the pieces, and she and her children build a good life. Vera finds a job at the public library. She makes many friends at work and at the Catholic church although she is no longer allowed to take communion because she is a divorced woman. It is a big point of unrest for Vera. She knows now she tried as hard as she could to make the marriage work and feels this treatment from the church is harsh.

Vera still enjoys entertaining, and she loves giving large sit down dinner parties. Her parties are like her mother's parties-- second to none. The food is awesome, and the guests are fun and entertaining. Through the years, she has learned to grow and to process most of the food she serves. Friends are amazed how much work this little lady can accomplish with relative ease. Vera is finally comfortable in her own skin like never before in her life.

Chapter 17

After a few years, Arthur remarries and comes back to Blair. It makes things uncomfortable for Vera at family functions. Her children are part of the family, but she just does not belong. As her children become independent adults, she decides it is time for her to move and to start a life of her own. She wants to be near her grandchildren, so she buys a house just a block and a half from Will and Elaine in Austin, Texas. Built by a local superintendent of schools, it is a sprawling home with a glass-enclosed patio, a large dining room for entertaining, and two living rooms. The fenced backyard includes most of a city block, plenty of room for her Great Pyrenees to run and to play with her kitties and her little Chihuahua. She builds a large bird house for her Cockatiels and yellow heads. She has always loved animals and feels accepted and loved when she is around them.

Will flies a helicopter for an independent oil company in the Yegua Creek basin about 60 miles east of Austin. Elaine works for the post office. Vera and Elaine start planning trips. Sometimes Will goes with them, sometimes they go by themselves, but they always have a lot of fun. Life is good. They take a trip to Chili during the time when the national news media was focusing on the huge forest fires in Mexico. To make small talk from the airport to their rooms, Elaine asks their cab driver, "Do you'll get any of that smoke here from Mexico?" She noticed in the rear view mirror he looked at her kind of strangely, but she dismisses it as a language problem. A couple of hours later there is a knock on their hotel room door, and there is the cabby to sell her some of that "Smoke from Mexico."

Elaine laughs her contagious laugh until the cabby finally leaves. This becomes a standing joke between Vera and Elaine.

To be around people, Vera gets a part time job at the local library. However, she cannot get interested in the local Catholic church. She has a bad taste in her mouth from the last church that made her feel like an outcast because she was divorced.

Vera meets Jess Mathis, a man about her age. He looks like an old hippie and rides a Harley. Elaine tells Vera to be careful because he might be trouble. Vera says, "I am not going to get remarried any time soon; I have learned my lesson." As the family gets to know Jess, they grow to love everything about the man. He is good to Vera, and he is so special with Will's three children. He is the grandfather they have always wanted. Jess spends hours playing with the children and the dogs; he is a kid at heart.

Many evenings Vera makes a big meal. Will, Elaine, and the kids come and stay until bed time to play games and laugh. Vera, Will, and Elaine sit on the back deck and watch the impromptu games and fun. Jess moves in with Vera, and by this time, it is fine with all the family. Life for Vera is good once again.

As time goes on, Jess and Vera start talking about celebrating their first anniversary of being together. A few days later, without any warning, Jess dies of a heart attack. He had gone to the store on his bike, walked back into the house, and fell dead right in front of Vera. The grandchildren have such strong wonderful memories of Jess at Vera's house, so for a while, they have a hard time coming to her house. Vera is alone once again.

Elaine's extended family lives near Lake Somerville and Deanville. They are a family full of laughter and fun. They love to see Vera coming along with Will and Elaine since she is always so much fun. At one of these occasions, she meets Jack Jorg, a family friend from Yegua Creek. Will is working in the Yegua Creek Basin, so he knows a lot about the people in the area. He knows Jack as a flamboyant, fun-loving, successful bachelor, who has lots of land, cattle, and several producing oil wells. Jack works hard and plays hard, a real colorful character.

He and Vera strike up a relationship. They are both short in statue. When Vera wears her high heels, they are the same height. He loves to dance, and he treats her like she is a China doll. He has such beautiful old fashioned manners. As a single man, he has partied hardily throughout the years, but his shenanigans have harmed no one. After only a few drinks, he gets tipsy and is the life of the party. A few more drinks, and he is the laughing stock of the party.

Jack is loved by all the residents of the area as a hard-working, fun-loving gentle man. Everyone is happy Jack has someone special in his life, but Yegua Creek is a town with a vicious tongue. Vera's son Will's last name is different then her last name, so they know she has been married twice already, something frowned upon heavily in this area. She also has a lot more money than almost everyone in Yegua Creek, so they assume she got her money from burying the first two husbands. The talk soon has her setting her eyes on cleaning out Jack's money. They figure, surely no one would really be interested in Ol' Jack. It is a sad commentary on an intelligent, hard-working, fun-loving man. Until he had Vera in his life, he just never had an opportunity to indulge his appreciation of the finer things in life like art, traveling, and music.

Jack takes Vera to Yegua Creek to meet his family. It is uncanny how much his sister Lillian "Lil" looks like Hettie, Vera's deceased sister. She is short in statue, has the same ruddy complexion, and the similarities in their facial features are uncanny. Lil's husband died many years before, and her son

Donald has taken over the family farm, living right next door to Lil. When he has a little extra time, Donald helps Uncle Jack with the cattle on his ranches. He is especially handy when Vera and Jack go on trips, taking care of everything while they are gone.

Now that Lil is retired from hairdressing, she spends a lot of her time at the Books for the Blind organization and at her little Lutheran church. Vera and Lil find they enjoy working together on the Books for the Blind's projects of assembling brail books and being very active in the church. Vera grew up being an active member of a church, and she has missed having a church home. She feels the Catholic church turned its back on her when she got divorced, but this little church family is so welcoming and loving.

Jack asks Vera to marry him. They make such a lovely couple, like they had been made for each other. Several years before, Jack built a new house right in the town of Yegua Creek. His new house is a long ranch-style house built on a slab, a really beautiful red brick with a two-car garage. A local carpenter built the house. It is a big house for only him, but when he asks Vera to marry him, they realize with all her treasures, they will need to add on to the house. He is so proud of all her treasures. He always says, "You just won't believe all the wonderful things she has in her house!" Vera has the money from the sale of Papa's villa in Prague to build the addition.

Evidently, no one knew, or if they did, they disregarded the information, but a huge fault line runs under the house. When they decide to add on to the house, they hire the same carpenter. The new plans convert the original double garage into a living room and dining room. They add extra rooms and another huge garage, making the house exceptionally long. Almost from the get go, the new addition is a fiasco. The floors crack, causing the floor tiles to pop off and the walls to move.

The exterior bricks crack, and some pieces fall off the house. It is a continual source of problems for the newlyweds, but they are happy.

Vera keeps her house in Austin. Will already has several rent houses, so he also rents her house to University of Texas students. It is a really good situation and a great monthly cash flow.

Vera and Jack join several local dance groups in the area; they get invites to dances about twice a month. It is a popular new idea for 10 to 12 couples to get together to split the cost to rent a dance hall and hire a band. Each couple invites 10 to 15 couples. In turn, every couple invited will take a turn to be the host sometimes during the year. In an area where social gathering has always been restricted to weddings and anniversaries, this new concept is a real social blessing. Vera enjoys Jack's family; his sister and nieces and nephews are her family. She has so many friends that she quickly becomes part of the community, and she is a refreshing addition to the small town. One of Vera's good friends Florice affectionately likes to say, "Vera is a big fish swimming in a small pond."

Vera and Jack also enjoy traveling. Jack especially enjoys having a companion, and he is so proud of all her accomplishments and her ability to speak so many languages. They are living the good life. A local travel agency is sponsoring a trip to China, and Jack, Vera, Will, and Elaine decide to go with the intention of traveling to the brewery if they can make the arrangements.

Vera is surprised the Chinese people are so different, so modern and up to date, from the last time she was here. The beggars are not on the streets, at least on the streets the tour traveled. One day the four of them leave the tour group and visit the brewery. They find the brewery almost as Vera remembered it from years ago. They are welcomed like royalty by the workers. A few of the older workers can remember her and her family. Other workers can only remember their families talking about her father Joseph; they still call him the "White Ghost." Evidently he had quietly helped many people, preferring to remain anonymous if at all possible. His generosity had become a legend, and the entire experience at the brewery makes it a trip to remember.

Several years later, in one of her history classes at Southwest Texas University in San Marcos, Will's daughter Kathy learns how to trace family history. She puts Will's daddy's name, Wally Wagner, into the computer. From the Salvation Army, up pops his information. He is living in Canada, just across the U.S. border near the Great Lakes. She gets his address, and together Will and Elaine write him a long letter. By return mail, they get the reply Will has been wanting for since he was 15-years-old. Wally is alive, active, and healthy. The long letter is written by Erika "Ery," Wally's wife since 1951. Ery writes the letter because about 11 years ago, Wally lost most of his vision to myopic degeneration and a blood clot behind the eye that cannot be eliminated.

In the letter (a shortened version of Wally's actual words), he tells Will (and Vera) in chronological order what happened in the 42 years after he left Peking.

Dear Will,

The trip from Peking to the old Taku Forts was like any regular railway trip. At the station in Taku is where the trouble began. The U.S. Army stationed there thinks we are hardboiled Nazis and treat us accordingly. We have not eaten all day. We are herded into a big Godown with only a small mobile water tank. We do not have cups, so we have to drink out of the two-inch tap, which is very difficult for small children. They are very thirsty and almost choke.

Early the next morning, we are loaded on LSTS and shipped out to the SS Marine Robin. They treat us ok. In Shanghai we pick up more people. As our ship leaves port, the U.S. Army band plays "Gonna take A Sentimental Journey." By this time the Army has figured out we are harmless civilians. As we reach the North Sea Channel, we are in the first ship; the second ship captain thinks he knows how to navigate the mines in the channel. When that ship strikes a mine, it is blown to smithereens and sinks. Our captain is a little white around the nose, so he asks if anyone on board our ship knows anything about the mine field. One man aboard says he has run the blockage 12 times successfully. Under his command, we sail into Bremerhaven. I did not know for years that Vera had been notified I died on the ship that sank.

Here our luck changes again, and the Army turns us over to a Polish soldier in a black uniform. The treatment is tough as we are herded into cattle cars (locked up). Away we go to Ludwigsburg. The trip takes two days, and we are without food or water. When we complain, we are told that is how the Germans treated them and for us to shut up.

In Ludwigsburg, we are moved into an old penitentiary on a small hill. The next morning we can walk around. One young man, a clerk from the consulate in Tientsin, has been with me all the way from Peking. He was raised in Ludwigsburg and wants to show one of his friends his father's house in the valley.

Without any warning, they are both shot to death like stray dogs. The Polish guards say there is a big sign to stay five meters away from the barbed wire. We never saw the sign, so it must have been on the outside of the fence. I promise myself I will get out of here as soon as possible. After about a month, we are released. A friend from our group has a sister living in the area; he invites me to live with them. However, I can not get a billeting permit. Without a billeting permit I do not exist for the food ration cards. There are four of us in the house living on three ration cards. One ration card is for 800 calories per person per day, dividing the total by four leaves 600 calories each, which is not enough for a grown person to survive. In the loft in the barn, I find a rifle. Each morning I go hunting, and for several days I am lucky enough to shoot three or four rabbits. We eat well for several days.

On Sunday morning, I go hunting as usual. I shoot four rabbits again, but someone reported the bang of the gun. When I walk around some willow bushes, I walk smack into two red caps (British MP's) sitting in a jeep. They tell me politely to hand over the gun and the rabbits. They start to ask, "Who are you?" My Tientsin British Emergency Corps' weapons carrier card did the trick. "From China, eh? Where is Victoria Road? The Race Course? The Astor House Hotel?" When I answer correctly, it convinces the one of them who has been in Tiensin that I am ok. They keep the gun and two rabbits and let me go.

After this experience, I figure I better leave. I tell my hosts, "China, here I come, or should this be impossible, Canada or USA here I come! Germany is out for me!"

I travel to Aachen and hang around the railway station to find out how to cross the border clandestine into Belgium. The general idea is to get to Antwerp, stow away on a boat, and hope for the best. There I meet Shorty from Tientsin, who also wants to skedaddle. We find out where to get a guide, and we pay 50 marks down and wait in front of the railroad station for the guide. We are made suckers as nobody shows up.

Then we get going ourselves and agree to write to "General Delivery" in Antwerp in case we get separated. Amongst the barbed wire, border guards, and cows, we get separated. My information has been that if you get across, mingle into a crowd. The cows do not want to mingle with me, but I get across anyway. I jump a freight and in ten minutes, pass a circus. Mingle in the crowd! I jump and find work at electric car ride. When they close, my boss tells me to come back tomorrow. Then he gives me a glad eye and asks, "No work papers?" I nod.

He tells me what he will pay me. The circus gives breakfast and supper, and I can sleep with the horses. He will talk to the boss. They give me a brown leather jacket, brown turtle neck, and a brown beret to wear with the brown woolen pants Vera sewed for me in Peking. I think I look very respectable with my razor and toothbrush in my pocket.

Sleeping on the straw bales with the horses was fine, but the elephants were so noisy it was hard to sleep. One night I was rudely awakened by the Elephant trainer. He showed me a camp cot and blankets right in front of the elephants. He said, "You sleep there; you snore good. Beasts like that and are real happy, no more noise!" He is right! When the elephants can see where the snoring is coming from, they stop making their noise and sleep. I get along real well with the elephants

I check in Antwerp; there is no mail from Shorty. He must have been caught. I check the vessels too, but none going to China. In the meantime, I convert my pay into U.S. dollars, and I am ready to go. Finally, there is a ship going to Shanghai. I get hired on as stevedore. I really work hard and then hide under a pile of ropes before the ship is to cast off. Along with some food, I even have my little bucket along to use for bodily functions. I have been warned to bring a bucket otherwise the urine will make a rusty trail, giving away my hiding place. There is a delay, and being dog tired, I fall asleep. The elephants would have loved it, but my snoring gave me away. I am discovered and taken to the captain. He is British, and I show him my TBEMC papers. He says he can call the harbor police and I will go to jail, or I can slip from board and disappear and not give him any trouble. I slunk away back to the elephants and horses. This can not go on forever.

After about a week, I say ta-ta to my boss and cross the clandestine border back. Here I run into trouble as I do not know that on account of the many clandestine border crossings, the whole area is out of bounds. As I pass the Last Inn (beer house) I wonder to myself, "Already the Inn is dark at 11 p.m." I remember the name though in case I will be asked where I came from. Sure enough within ten minutes, I hear a German border guard shout, "Halt, wer geht da?" I try to convince the soldiers I am a local on my way home after having too much liquid sunshine. I am trying to use being drunk as a reason I cannot explain exactly where I am going. I think I am doing pretty fine with the story. The soldiers are laughing at my antics, and I think they are warming up to our conversation. They ask where I had been drinking.

I say, "At the Last Inn." When they ask if I broke in, I reply, "No, I did not!"

"Funny," says one guard. "That place has been closed for two months." I sit in that small border point for about 10 days till they establish my identity.

Now back to Seppensen, I decide to get the papers I need, so I went into the U.S. zone to get billeting permits and whatever went with it. I had been born in Hamburg, Germany, in 1919 but went to China when I was three. Since I am not listed in Germany in 1939, I am considered a refugee and have to stay in a refugee camp behind barbed wire and clear the ruins for three months. Nobody wants to do this coolie work. Neither do I, so I escape.

My next trip takes me to Loerrach at the Swiss border. I am a lot smarter now crossing borders. No baggage, and while running through the wet grass, my pants are rolled up high since wet pant legs are a dead give away. A good set of wire cutters is a must. What a difference within 200 meters.

Everything is well lit, no broken windows, and I can buy to eat whatever my heart desires. A hotel to my liking is soon found, and I immediately send a cable to my father asking him to send me $500 by cable. My Tante Christa tells me my father did receive the cable from Switzerland; however, he thought it was a fake as no German could leave Germany legally. Therefore no money. I draw a total blank when I try to remember my father-in-law's friends in Zürich. I take the French exit back to Germany. As I am a top hand at border crossings, I encounter no problems. This all might sound funny now, but it was dead serious then as people got shot to death crossing the border. On my way north, I traverse the Black Forest. In Villingen, the UNRRA is looking for people who can speak German, English, and French. They like my nose, and I am hired, putting together convoys of Poles wanting to return to Poland. They are in the French-occupied territory, and the French want them out. When this transit camp closes, I have enough money to give escape another try. After talking to so many Poles that really have been around, Italy looks like the real spot. Crossing the border at Mittenwald (U.S. Zone) into Austria (French Zone) is pretty tricky as the snow is almost waist deep, and one got completely soaked. A farmer gives me permission to dry up in his barn, and he also feeds me since I must look very frozen.

From there, I walk all the way through Austria to the Brenner Pass. Here I get together with some smugglers, and away we went. I can hardly keep up with them in the deep snow. I made it however and boarded a train to Rome. Near Rome in Cinecita is a huge refugee camp for Chinese looked after by the Chinese Embassy in Rome. They tell me because of political unrest in China, there will not be a ship to China for at least a year. I head for Genoa to look for a ship. On the way, I go through Rome and think, "Might as well look at the Vatican as I will never pass by here again." The treasures in the Vatican are fabulous. When I walk back out on the street, a Caribinieri Patrol stops me. "Documenti *per favoure!" Reaching for them, I freeze. No papers! My money and papers had been lifted off me in the Vatican! No amount of protesting helps. I am tall and blond, therefore "SS." The Regina Coelli, which means Queen of Heaven, takes me into her arms. This is the main prison in Rome.*

A couple days later, the trip to Monte Casino starts. We have a tough time. Always five men on ankle chains clear the rubble of the Old Fort which had been fought for so bitterly in the war. After about a month, I have enough money to buy a stamp to send a letter to China to get new, correct ID papers.

One day as the five of us chained together sit there on a break, my eyes pop out. Who is lead in there in chains? Shorty! He pretty near flips! He says, "I heard you left for China via Italy, so I tried too."

After eight months in that hell hole, my papers arrive, and I am released, naturally back to Germany. It is very frustrating.

Now with my new papers from China, I make up my mind to do things legally. In Bremen, I finally receive a billeting permit under great difficulties. As I have to go to the Captain of the MP's of the Army, I have to go to the "Polizeipraesidium," which means police station. Looking for the captain's office, I have to read all names on the bulletin board. Can you beat that a sign read: Uebersetzer Buero: Ernst Wagner. Can that be my lost uncle? Up I go and knock at the door and hear the familiar voice, "Come in!" It is Uncle Ernst.

When he sees me, he turns white as a sheet. All he can say is, "You're alive!" As we talk, I begin to wish I had never opened his door. He tells me I had been reported dead. As he talks, my whole world falls in on me. He tells me how the whole family grieved over my death, especially my father and Vera. They were such a comfort to each other. I notice he is making a special effort to tell me how much Vera grieved over my death. That does not surprise me; I know she loves me with all her heart. He tells me my father had also been repatriated to Germany. With great compassion, he informs me my father died in prison in Germany. By this time, my head is swimming. Then he brings up the subject of how much turmoil there is in China. How everything is changing because of the struggle for power. I begin to feel there is something even worse he has not told me. When I ask about Vera and Will, he says he lost direct communication with them after my father left China. When I ask him directly what he knows about them, he continues. He knows Vera's parents escaped just before the Communists took control, but he thinks Vera might have married a Marine Lieutenant from Texas, but he is not sure. He also is not sure, but he thinks she got out of China before the Communists took over. I ask if he knows his name. He can not remember. I ask, "Is his name Martin Friedel?" He says that does sound familiar. I remember him as a good family friend before I left China. In one short visit, my whole life has turned up side down. All my reasons for wanting to go back to China are gone. My dad is gone, and Vera and Will probably no longer live there. Maybe that is why all my attempts to get there have failed.

The next several days Uncle Ernst and I do some investigating and find Lieutenant Martin Friedel has been transferred to Camp Lejeune in North Carolina.

After more investigating, I have his home phone number.

It takes me several days to work up the courage to call the number; I pray this will all be some kind of mix up. When Vera's sweet voice answers the phone, I know she is now another man's wife. I can tell by her reaction when she hears my voice she had no idea I was still alive. Through tears she tells me she never thought she would hear my voice again. I explain what caused the confusion about the ship that was sunk. I tell her how I can not understand why my father did not send me any money when I telegrammed him. She tells me about that mix up and keeps saying how she wishes they had known I had sent that telegram. I can tell from the tone of her voice and the things she is saying that she still loves me, but she can't say all the things I waited so long to hear. And I cannot tell her all about the love in my heart. I can no longer talk. I tell her I am running out of money and will call her back in a few days when I can save more money.

The next time I call, she tells me she is remarried; I tell her I have already figured that out. She tells me how good Martin is to Will and how happy they are as a family. She says Martin had to adopt Will to get him to America, and they have not told Will he is adopted. When she tells me she is expecting his child, my heart brakes into a million pieces. My heart is breaking, and I am finding it impossible to continue to talk. I tell her the time is about up, and I will call back in a few days after I can have some time to think.

I cannot fault Vera for remarrying; she thought I was dead. As many times as I needed official paper work to get across borders, I fully understand the need for the adoption to get Will into U.S. Vera and my son are happy in a new life, and I have nothing to offer. I am barely able to keep food in my own mouth. I would not offer to share my life with a dog. I also know I would be barred from entering the U.S. I am sure a long distance relationship with Will would just confuse my son.

When I call Vera back, I tell her I will stay out of their lives. I tell her I will love her until the day I die. I will call now and then to find out about my son. When I hang up the phone, it is like starting a new life. I have no home, no family, and the future looks bleak. Everything I knew and love is no longer within my reach.

In post-war Germany, it is impossible for me to get a job as I have no German recommendations or references. It is understandable they pick their own boys for the jobs. I work as a street photographer. I even get stuck in an ice bear outfit for a fair, and the bear's head is very hot. Then I start work for the U.S. Army as a supervisor of a bowling alley. Here I meet Erika, a beautiful fun loving German girl, who loves to listen to and laugh at my stories.

The bowling alley closed or I quit; I can't remember. I hear about a ship that was hiring. When I got to the ship, the only job left was the steward's position. I talked the Captain into hiring me. I did not know the first thing about being a steward, but they were promising each person on the ship 1,500 calories a day. I was going to make it work. (Will, when we get together, I have many stories about my time on the ship to share.)

On my first time back in port, Erika "Ery" and I were married. It felt so right to have someone so gentle and kind in my life. While back at sea aboard the ship,

I got a letter from Ery that Germans could legally immigrate to Canada. That was it. I mustered off when we got back to Bremen, and I applied for immigration papers in Hannover, which is about a two hour trip from Bremen. Everybody said it would take half a year to be processed. Having learned my lesson by my various sorties, I marched past the line of about 50 people. I demanded in English from a German clerk to see the immigration officer. He was bluffed, and when somebody came out of the office, I was ushered in. That man never knew I jumped the line. Furthermore, when I got inside, I saw a schoolmate from Tientsin. He explained he was only working to see that his papers stayed on top of the pile. He confirmed he would do the same for me. When I went there a week later, he was gone already. Now I had to look for another helper. A girl there was very helpful. I told her I would send her a nice present if she would look after my papers. She did, and my papers came through quickly. Ery then sent her a Spanish hand-stitched shawl. Now I had to get my passport stamped. Nothing to it, I thought. However, for some unknown reason, I carried a stamp out of there that was not valid for Canada. What a mess! The officer told me it might take a month till I got a new passport, and I then should try again. He did not know I had an uncle in the police station. I saw him that afternoon and was told a new passport could be ready the next morning at eight a.m. for me to catch the 8:30 bus. Cost: 25 U.S. cigars out of the PX. This was arranged with some dealing at the railroad station. Hanover, here I come! Like usual, after submitting my passport, I had to wait five hours and take the next bus. They thought I had a fake passport, and they wanted to uncover the ring that sold them. Well, everybody in the end was all smiles.

Ery and I married in June, and in August I left for Quebec with Ery following in October. When I landed in Quebec, I was taken to Camp Ajax near Toronto and given a job in a lumber camp at the remote place of White River, Ontario. Ery got a job as a cookee a few miles further inland in a camp for about 100 men who went out daily to cut logs. She cleaned tables, floors, washed dishes and did other disagreeable chores. By the end of December, we had saved $700 dollars and set up housekeeping here in Canada.

When a big Tube Co. built a big plant here, I was hired as office manager. Ery got a good job as a bookkeeper for a local law firm. Things got better for us, and in 1957, we acquired our present home, a bungalow. Years rolled along, and on March 20, 1964, our one and only child Barbara was born. It was the happiest event in our lives. Ery became a full time housewife and mother, and we enjoyed our offspring immensely.

About 11 years ago, I lost most of my vision and became a member of the Canadian National Institute for the Blind. In addition to the myopic degeneration, there is a blood clot in the back of my eye that cannot be eliminated. I worked with my disability for seven years until I retired. I am now on the board of the CNIB and often work on fundraisers. I also volunteer at our local hospital to help the sick with their therapy treatments twice weekly.

This is enough for today, this will give you a good idea how I fared for about six years. More next time.

Will, Ery and I would like to begin making plans to meet with you and your lovely little family and also Vera either here or in Yegua Creek. While we are still in relatively good health, we think we would like to come to see you. As years go by, it may be necessary for you to come see us for visits.

With Love to all of you,
Wally

P. S. Special big hug for Kathy! We have been searching for Will for so long, and we think it is great that you have found us.

Soon plans are made for Wally and Ery to visit Yegua Creek in late March. They would get a break from the ice in Canada, and spring in Central Texas would make the perfect setting for a meeting. Elaine and Ery are as excited as their husbands in anticipation of the first meeting for Wally and Will.

However, Vera is in a quandary. She is so glad Will is going to get to spend time with his beloved father, but she knows people around Yegua Creek already don't think much of her for being married twice. Now they will figure out she was actually married three times. She also knows Jack will have a hard time with the fact she withheld the information from him from the start. They decide to have Wally and Jack together as little as possible. After all, Wally is coming to see Will, not Vera.

In March of 1988, Wally and Ery fly into Austin. Will flies the company helicopter to the airport to pick them up. When Will lays eyes on his father, it is like looking at an older version of himself. They are both tall and blond. Will is so intrigued by his father's exaggerated muscular forearms and calves, just like Popeye. Wally explains his overly defined lower extremity muscles are from the manual labor in the prisons. As he worked on the chain gangs clearing debris, he was always chained to other prisoners. They were either five men with leg chains or ten men with arm chains. It did not take long for Will at 55 to realize he could not beat his 77-year-old father arm wrestling.

When they meet, Wally is 77, Will 55, and Wally's daughter Barbara 33, each 22 years apart. They discover the phenomenon that whenever one of them had a double digit, they all had double digit ages. Wally 66, Will 44, Barbara 22; Wally 55, Will 33, and Barbara 11.

Their time together is spent in endless stories, catching up on 42 years apart. The stories Wally tells makes everyone laugh, and he has an uncanny knack for laughing at himself. In hind sight, he can see the ludicrous side of his actions even though at the times when they were happening, they were life and death struggles.

One night Wally shared the story he promised in his letter. "Will, you remember in my letter I said I would tell you more stories about my time on the Old English Ship as a steward I had no idea what a steward did on a ship, but since they were giving 1,500 calories a day, I was going to make it work.

As I left the ship after I was hired, I saw Captain Johann, a friend I met the night before at a beer hall. I have to trust someone, so I tell Captain Johann about my dilemma. The Captain tells me the next morning three venders will be coming to the ships dock to try to get the business of stocking the ship for the voyage. He tells me to pick one and tell him how many men will be on the ship and how long we will be out at sea. The vender will bring everything the ship needs for the trip, right down to the toothpicks. I follow his suggestion, and it works beautifully. I fake the rest with good manners and my gift of gab. I really enjoy the position on the ship.

Captain Johann turns out to be second-in-command on the ship. He had been a submarine captain in the war, but he has some red tape to clear before he can have the command of a commercial vessel. Until then, he needs work just like everyone else.

The ship is one of the first ships bought by Germans after the war; it was a British ship. It is in terrible shape, rusty and old. After we get underway, no matter how hard the crew tries, they cannot keep the metal flag up on the flag pole. All the holders have rusted off, so to keep the flag up on the pole, it has to be welded in place, making it stationary. They know it is against the rules to make a ships flag immovable, but while out at sea, it works great.

One day when we need fuel as we round a bend to enter a port, and low and behold, there is a huge U.S. fleet in the harbor. As we pass the first ship, the captain knows he is supposed to dip his flag in respect to the other ship, especially a military ship. Well, that is impossible with the flag welded on the pole. As we pass the first ship, they toot their horn, but we just keep going. After we pass the second ship without dipping the flag, the main ship in the fleet addresses us with a bull horn. The deep voice wants to know our ship's name and the captain's name. We knew they are taking our actions as a show of deliberate disrespect.

I did not understand why, but our reply gave Captain Johann's name as the captain instead of our real captain's name. There is a long silence from the flag ship. When the deep voice came back on the bull horn, in very ominous tones they notify Captain Johann they will be boarding our ship. The voice says everyone on board our ship will be transported to the flag ship immediately.

On board our old British ship, we find a book on British maritime conduct. In that book, it says it is an insult to blow a horn at a British ship. Our crew is going to use that as the reason we did not dip our flag. We know it is a flimsy excuse, but it is better than none.

When the crew boards, they do not ask for any explanation for the flag incident. I just know I am headed back to some kind of prison for some reason. That is how life has been for me for years. As we near the flag ship, we see the fleet captain is waiting for us at the gang way. When we got close enough to distinguish the fleet captain's features, Captain Johann gets white as a sheet; he recognizes the fleet captain. Captain Johann's submarine had sunk his ship to the bottom of the ocean during the war. We are all shaking in our boots.

When we reach the ship, the fleet captain walks up to Captain Johann, salutes him, shakes his hand with both of his hands, and hardily welcomes him onto his ship. The fleet captain is obviously overjoyed to see Captain Johann. He says he thought he would never get the chance to personally thank Captain Johann for being a humanitarian and a hero.

The fleet captain explains when Captain Johann's submarine sank his ship, he had been under direct orders from Hitler never to pick up any survivors. He was supposed to let them drown. At great risk to his ship and his career, Captain Johann surfaced his ship and rescued the crew from the ocean and took them to safety. The fleet captain throws Captain Johann and his crew one hell of a party."

Only one of Wally's stories has no humor, and the family listens carefully to his words. "In one prison one of the meanest guards has an exceptionally strong dislike for me and Shorty. He is always inflicting extra pain on us. We are pretty sure he is jealous of our close friendship. Together we can always find something to laugh about even in this hell hole. One day, along a deserted stretch of road, the guard hits me hard with a shovel. The blow lays open a gash on my forehead. Look here, the scar is still very visible today. As the guard raises the shovel to inflict another blow, I raise my arms to deflect the blow. My arms are stronger then the guard, so as the shovel comes down again, I am able to wrestle the shovel away from the guard. In the scuffle, I kill the guard. Several prisoners see what happens. All the prisoners chained together quickly help me roll the body down into a deep ditch. There are no regrets; it all happened so fast. Everyone knows once I got the shovel away from the guard, I really had no choice but to kill him. If I let him live, he surely would have retaliated against all of us ten fold. He was already making our lives a living hell. I know I will probably be shot for killing him, but I also know the guard left me no choice. Much to our surprise, that evening when the guard does not return to the compound, no one went looking for him. Evidently, he had been as hateful to the other guards as he had been to the prisoners. They are all glad he is gone. No one, prisoner or guard, ever mentions the incident."

When Wally and Jack meet, Jack keeps remarking how Will and Wally sure look a lot alike. Wally is still the life of the party, and Jack has always liked fun people. He likes to laugh, to drink a little beer, and to tell his own stories. Wally takes special effort to listen to Jack's stories, so they hit it off really well. They all spent the week with loads of laughter and good food. Everyone is sad when the week grows to a close.

During the week, Jack figures out that Will is Wally's son, and he feels betrayed, hurt, and then angry. Vera explains to Jack that she regrets never telling him about Wally. She had no intention of keeping it a secret, but in the beginning, it just was never the right time to tell him because she had so many husbands it sounded so bad. Then as time went on, it was too late to mention Wally without damaging their relationship. There never was a time to tell him without sounding like she had deliberately lied, which was not the case. Even though Jack understands Vera's motives, her unintentional lie is a point of contingency for a long time, mostly because he feels that people are laughing at him because now they know she had not been truthful with him. They finally get past the hurt, but their relationship is permanently damaged.

Chapter 18

Jack, Vera, and his sister Lil enjoy several more years of carefree living. After Vera and Jack had been married for about ten years, Vera and Lil notice a gradual change in Jack's behavior. At first the family just thinks it is the stress of the house literally falling apart. Soon they notice more and more hostility and anger. He begins to forbid Vera's children and grandchildren to visit in "his" home. When they do, he is openly unfriendly and hostile, making the visits extremely unpleasant. He also starts to accuse his nephew Donald, Lil's son, of stealing from him on the ranch. Soon Vera has to go to her children if she wants to visit with them. When she returns, he is always angry because she has left him alone. Alzheimer's is taking control of his mind, and life is no longer good in the Jorg home. Lil comes and helps Vera as much as she can, but she can't abide his continual accusations of Donald. For several years, the deterioration continues. Eventually, Vera is forced to take Jack to the Alzheimer's unit in a nearby nursing home.

The nursing home director asks Vera to stay away for a few days to see if he will improve without her visits. The nurses observe that when she comes, he always gets so worked up and cusses her up one side and down the other. They think maybe he will behave better without her visits, but it does not work. He just takes it out on the staff. Soon the management calls Vera; they are not going to be able to keep him. None of the staff is willing to work with him. Vera begs until they reach a compromise. They will keep him, but she will come twice a day to feed and to dress him. For almost two years, all her time is spent either coming or going to the nursing home. She endures his continual abuse until his death.

Jack had no will, so after his death, his wealth is divided by the rules of the state of Texas. Vera receives enough from the proceeds of the sale of his land and the house (what was left of it) to live a very comfortable life, and she and the family are still friends after the divisions of Jack's property. Vera takes her collection and moves back to her house in Austin. By this time, a neighborhood not far from her house has deteriorated noticeably, and when she tries to get her collection covered by insurance, she is told the only way any company will insure her collection is for her to have an around the clock armed guard.

She and Will decide the only thing they can do is install an elaborate alarm system with a gate across the driveway. The security company does a great job of monitoring her units. Just as when her treasures arrived in Robsville so many years before, the Chinese mystique or air of mystery and intrigue help to keep people at a distance. Vera giggles, "Maybe my enormous collection of Buddha gods gives me some protection."

Will is working off shore flying a helicopter to take workers to and from off shore oil rigs in the Gulf of Mexico. He is home a month and then is gone a month. Often Vera, Elaine, and Will travel together, and sometimes Vera and Elaine go on trips while Will is away on his job. Vera gets to enjoy her grandchildren as they grow into adulthood. In her later years, Vera retains her adventuresome spirit. She loves to try new things. Her favorite saying is, "If you don't try it, how will you know if you will like it?" She tells about trying and liking the 100-year-old eggs that she ate when she lived in China. She says, "They were very good." She would never have known how delicious they were if she hadn't been adventurous enough to try something new.

For Will's 60th birthday, all three go to Canada to visit Wally. This is the first birthday Will gets to celebrate with his mother and father. On that day, if fate had not torn them apart, Wally and Vera would have already celebrated their 60th wedding anniversary. They all have so much fun together. Will gets to meet his half sister and Wally's (and his) extended families. Vera and Wally's wife, Ery, became best friends when they met in Yegua Creek years before. Vera is so glad Wally found someone who is good to him. Vera feels Wally had been cheated out of so much, especially being part of Will's life.

As the years pass by, age begins to steal Vera's ability to live alone. At first her granddaughter comes and lives with her, but Kathy has a life to live, and Vera begins to need more care as Alzheimer's claims her mind. Elaine and Will are not far from retiring, but they are both still working. With Will leaving for extended periods of time, Elaine carries all the responsibility. Vera closes up her house in Austin and moves in with Joanie and her family in Blair.

When it becomes apparent Vera will never be returning to live in Austin, the family holds a huge estate auction. There is a front-page story in the local paper with a picture of Will and Elaine standing in front of the gold threaded tapestry Joseph received from the emperor. The story tells about the exquisite treasures being offered for auction. They get a few Chinese art collectors from Houston, but most of the buyers are just curious people from the Austin area. By this time, Alzheimer's has deteriorated Vera's mind, and she will not understand why they are selling her prized possessions. The children know she will only know enough to be sad, so they do not bring her to the sale.

Vera dies several years later at the age of 88 after spending her last years living with her daughter. She lived a long life full of love, life, laughter, and tragedy. She left behind four beautiful well-rounded children and their families that love each other's company and spend a lot of quality family time together.

Vera's obituary in the paper read:

Surrounded by her loving family, Vera Jorg went peacefully into the arms of her Savior on November 22, 2009.

Vera was born in Peking China May 23, 1921. Her Austrian father owned a brewery in Russia until the family fled across Siberia to China, escaping the turmoil preceding the Russian Revolution. In Peking, her father established the Five Star Brewery that is still in existence today. Vera was the only surviving child of four but had a happy life and wonderful home in China. Sponsored by a philanthropist, she attended the American School in Peking. She was valedictorian of her class and won awards for her excellence in the Chinese language. She was sent to Europe for part of her schooling and became proficient in several languages there. She attended Peking University for two years prior to her marriage.

She lived all over the world, making her home in Texas where she raised her family. Vera's greatest joy in life was her family and friends. At a young age, she developed a passion for animals of all kinds, opening her home and heart to many. She also enjoyed ballroom dancing, bowling, crafts, gardening, traveling, and displaying her lovely Chinese antiques. She volunteered countless hours with her Lutheran church friends constructing books for the blind.

Vera is survived by her three sons and their wives and one daughter and her husband. She was also blessed with 13 grandchildren and 15 great-grandchildren.

If fate had not intervened and forced them to get a "friendly divorce," Vera and Wally would have been married 68 years in 2009. What the obituary does not say is Vera died on November 22, Wally's birthday, and Wally died two weeks later.

They are together at last!

CPSIA information can be obtained at www.ICGtesting.com
Printed in the USA
LVOW090837220512

282765LV00001B/10/P

9 781935 909279